THE TALK

Black, White and Brown People Learning from Each Other

America's Greatest Fear

DONALD PAYNE

PAYING HOMAGE

Believe it or not, I owe the conception of this book to a 76-year-old white lady who demanded daily that I write down my thoughts. She swore that my experiences, information, and conversations with others mattered.

The two-way dialogue we engaged in had a significant impact on both of us in learning, understanding, and agreeing to disagree with love. SN... this is for you.

To my family on both my mother's and father's sides. All that I am is because of all that you were. I owe a debt that can never be repaid to you, so I am attempting to pay it forward by sharing thoughts, experiences, and information with others.

If you are reading this, I pay homage to you for being open enough to simply give another person's point of view a moment of your time.

"A moment of a person's time can lead to a lifetime of change."

DP
Thank you.

TABLE OF CONTENTS

INTROLUDE

I am not a saint; I am not an expert on anything other than my life. By expert, I mean that I am aware of my own life experiences and the impact those experiences have on me. At no point do I claim to be a scholar or better than the next person. There is no question as to whether I am flawed; I am. It is a fact that I have had substantial failures and huge mistakes in my life. My ability to learn from those mistakes, listen to others and recognize that changes that are made to my behavior can do wonders for me in the future are attributes that have sustained me in tough times.

Observing human beings, having curious conversations, and engaging in controversial debates are some of my favorite things to do. I have been like this since I was a young boy. (I also love playing chess and getting beat. Learning from losses allowed me to look at my thought process, adjust and come back later to obliterate my opponent.

One of the best aspects of my childhood was being surrounded by elders. Listening, learning, and talking with them provided me with a subconscious perspective I did not realize I possessed for years. Life experiences and exposure to different types of people are also major contributors to the opinions I have formulated over time. These early experiences, combined with my desire not to simply accept information I am told but to research data from multiple sources, are a big part of how I have drawn my own conclusions about most topics in life.

Over the years, I have learned that data can be manipulated to the benefit of whoever is presenting the information. History has been erased, rewritten, misrepresented and often just outright lied about. Sifting through those obstacles for the truth can be incredibly challenging for anyone to complete. As an adult, I can see how accepting the truth vs what we have been told can be more difficult for some than others, for many reasons. I find that the main obstacle in seeing truth usually comes down to our individual fears of self-reflection.

I am a father, husband, brother, son, uncle, grandfather, cousin, nephew, stepdad, divorcee, sinner, spiritual, loving, type C Personality Virgo. Throughout life, I did many stupid things that could have and probably should have resulted in death. Thanks to the father above, he saw fit not to take me back then.

My political affiliation or strategy has been very simple for most of my life. Simply, take stock in the people who take stock in you.

I realize that Democratic and Republican leaders play the exact same games with their constituencies, just on different sides of a fence.

At times, I have major problems with Democrats, and other times it is with Republicans. Based on my research, these parties care more about their own interests than they do about the average American citizen who puts them in office.

I believe in the concept of true law and order with equal justice for all. Fair treatment for everyone via equal rights, supported by a judicial system with laws that are applied with consistency to all citizens regardless of race, color, status, or creed. Though I believe in these things fundamentally, I know that we do not execute these concepts consistently or correctly in our country.

Opportunities in life should be awarded to those that put in the work to get them.

I do not believe in the good old boy system for any of us. Likewise, I don't believe in doors being closed off to someone just because of how they look or don't look. Differences are good things when it comes to success and growth.

Overall, this book comes to you from someone who has experienced failure and success. Someone who knows what it is like to be broke and hungry. Also, as someone who has learned what it's like to have more than one needs. Let's be clear, though, I do not know what it is like to be wealthy; therefore, I do not try to speak on that concept. It is important to recognize that one can have an opinion; however, that opinion is automatically limited when one has not walked in the shoes of the subject being discussed.

It is my hope that having a conversation with you about who I am, how I think, and some of my life experiences just might tear down a few barriers between us. Being open to different opinions and accepting additional facts you may not have known or believed are huge steps to understanding yourself and others. Who knows, it may even prompt you to not just absorb what you read here, but to physically sit down with someone completely different from you. For me, this perspective is true learning. It's had an enormous impact on my life.

Please allow me to be transparent with you. As a Black man, I am fully aware that I have experiences that some of you cannot ever truly understand. That is not an insult; it's simply the fact that sometimes we cannot walk in another person's shoes. I recognize that this is also the space I stand in with others who have had journeys that differ from my own. Nonetheless, these kinds of engagement experiences have shaped my life, but they are not the only things in my life. Every black man's experience is specific to him and his life, as it is with any other human being. Again, my experiences and thoughts are just that…. mine. I'm sure I share some similarities with other black men and those not black in some facets, and in other situations, I'm sure that I do not. We can never know any of these differences or similarities if we refuse to talk, share, and listen. Perhaps for a short time, we can enter each other's space and look at life through an alternate lens.

POWER -THE BEGINNING AND THE END

One of the many definitions of Power is stated as follows: political or social authority or control, especially that exercised by a government. Another definition is the capacity or ability to direct or influence the behavior of others or the course of events. The origin of the Power is derived from the Anglo-Norman French Poeir, from an alteration of Latin Posse, which means "be able".

As a toddler, I did not have a complete understanding of the concept of power; however, I did quickly understand the principle of "the ability" to do things. A child finds out very quickly how much power they lack physically when they attempt to do the same things they see adults doing. Moving a chair out of the way, picking up a bag or opening and closing a heavy door.

I remember specifically being 3 years old and testing my "power". After eating dinner one evening in my highchair, I decided dinner was over and wanted to get down. My mother was in the process of cleaning up the kitchen and was not ready to take me out of the chair.

First, I became annoyed with waiting for her to get me out. Next, I proceeded to try and unfasten the belts that restricted me from getting out of the chair. Of course, I could not undo the secure process my mother implemented to keep me safe, which elevated my frustration and anger. Since I did not have the power to free myself from the chair, I did the next best thing I could think of. In an angry fit, I began rocking the chair back and forth frantically and before my mother could get to me, guess what happened?

The good news was that I didn't have a concussion, but I hurt myself, leaving a lovely goose egg on my head. Even as a toddler, I so desperately wanted the power to control my own actions that when I couldn't get it, I put myself in harm's way to try to assert any power I could. Looking back, this was a very telling innate characteristic about human beings and power. Even as a child, I learned quickly that power or lack thereof had an immense impact on life. Power is the key to doing what you want, getting what you need, and acquiring what you desire. Thus, smacking my head on the ground from that highchair was the perfect illustration of how far one will go to satisfy their desires. The revelations that came to me as a toddler, even then, were very simple. Number one, the power that things can have over you at times can feel inescapable. Two, the drive that human beings experience to apply their own power is often stronger than accepting the feeling of being unable to change things. These are two of the major struggles mankind has seemed to have been embattled with for centuries.

History speaks volumes about those who wielded power over others at all costs. It also speaks to individuals who were committed to never accepting giving that kind of control to those ruling over them. This explains many of the historic battles that accompanied those mindsets. This concept around the power struggle has remained true from centuries past to now. If you doubt that or are not aware of these conflicts, just check the fall of the Roman Empire, the civil war, WW1, WW2, Vietnam conflict, Syria, Iran, Iraq, Israel, Palestine and many more.

Just for a moment, imagine the journey of walking through this life with minimal options to positively change the environment that those in power have imposed upon you. My friends… that has been the fate of many cultures all around the globe.

To be more specific, that is very much the fate I have often felt all of my life, along with 46 million other people who look like me in the United States of America.

If you have ever felt moments of helplessness and powerlessness, you know how terrible it is. Knowing how you will be treated when your drive to not concede or give up your power (otherwise stated as bucking the system) kicks in can be terrifying. While it is always liberating to stand up for your humanity and what is right, the reality of those consequences doesn't feel so liberating. Living with that feeling of what will happen if you stand up for yourself 24 hours a day, as most people in my shoes do, is what I am asking you to consider.

I believe that most organizations begin with one or more people in a group who are in charge. In the inception of that organization, that person or persons have the power to determine the image, infrastructure, laws of operating laws, expectations, beneficiaries, and distribution of profits. If the organization succeeds and grows exponentially, these individuals take credit for the foundational framework that it began with. They are the primary beneficiaries of that success.

The United States of America is no exception to this rule, as it also began as an organization. We often speak of the Founding

Fathers' vision of what this nation would become and the foresight we believe they had in forging laws to govern us by. Those laws are mainly based on the constitution officially.

Typically, in companies or organizations, the establishment of power and who actually holds it tends to be a good thing to establish hierarchy and order. However, in a country that houses different cultures, races and persons with varying religious beliefs, it tends not to be such a good thing when the holder of power is not diverse or doesn't see diversity as a strength. The forefathers didn't belong to most of these categories just listed. They belonged to a specific group that created guidelines for those who also fit into that specific group. All persons outside of these rule makers' culture, race and religion really didn't have a constitution.

Very simply, in most scenarios, if you are not part of the original plan or included in the original plan favorably, you will likely always be on the outside of the organization, hoping for that policy and or process to one day apply to you. Being on the outside of a power structure or not being included in a structure can all be an awful existence. What I have come to realize is that those who are on the inside of any power structure are the ones who have the privilege of that structure, no matter what level they are at inside the structure.

Personally, I do not deem the concept of privilege to simply be a "white person's" status globally. However, I will say that specifically in America, minorities are and have always been outside of the power structure. Minorities were not included as benefactors of the foundational origins of this society back in historical 1776 or prior to that, we were property. Like it or not, that means that minorities were not intended to have those same privileges as those who were a part of this structure or those who created the United States of America.

My hope would be that individuals (yes, this means white people also) would not get so offended when the "privilege" conversation arises. It's not an attack or a negative indictment of all white people as a basic concept. Nor does it imply that you are rich, poor, hardworking or lazy, had an easy life or a hard one. It simply identifies that you are a benefactor of being included in the system or structure as it was designed. It means that you have certain liberties (whether you take them or not) that were created and designed for you as someone, inclusive of the structure. As with any benefits or options in life, there are those that choose to take advantage of those options negatively and flaunt them in the face of others or use those options as a weapon. The individuals who operate this way will almost always be offended by this conversation, no matter what.

One would think that the feeling of being offended is a defense mechanism rooted in the acknowledgment of flaws in the structure or organization. More times than not, with privilege, the feeling of being offended is often rooted in the fact that the individual is conscious of the role they have, knowing or unknowingly, in negatively impacting others who do not benefit from America's structure.

Witnessing what privilege was from the viewpoint of a teenager brought about some of the hardest lessons I had ever seen. It also indoctrinated me into what I later understood as the game of life. Lessons that I still watch and participate in today. Prior to the teenage years, the concept of privilege and what it meant was simply something I didn't fully understand. The joy of being a child, oblivious to many of these tainted ways, is a gift you don't realize you have. Once I reached an age to understand the concept of people being inside of an organization, or better yet, being on the outside of it, the experiences in those early years were extremely impactful to me. So many of life's critical moldings happen in these early years that later in life, you look back and comprehend what you learned or were exposed to. It seemed trivial to me at the time as a kid, but I actually remember something as simple as being in kindergarten and first learning how to write. I remember that I was one of two left-handed students in my class. I now realize that my teacher simply didn't know how to teach a left-handed person how to write; however, back then, the way she decided to handle the situation, instead of admitting she didn't know what to do, really sucked.

My teacher decided that by the power vested in her, she would convert me to being right-handed, and she put a cardboard box on my left arm to restrict me from using it. This was the solution my teacher felt would resolve what she deemed was my defect and get me on track. By the time I told my mother what was going on (who immediately went to the school), the year was almost over. Truth be told, I didn't complain about it all as I just accepted what was happening as well as what the rules were. My mother and I were having a conversation in passing one day about school, and I mentioned what was going on. What happened when my mother found this out is a whole other story in itself; let's just say the school had a bad day.

The point was that my teacher believed she had the power and the privilege to do something to me in a manner she wouldn't have done to other children in class. This did not happen to other kids who didn't look like me without permission from their parents. Because I didn't know any better, there was nothing wrong with the system, and I accepted that behavior from the person in power.

You may be thinking that this is not a power or privilege issue. More so, the teacher would have done the same thing to other children simply because she didn't know how to teach someone left-handed, right? As a child, I didn't think anything of it either. As an adult, I later learned what it really meant that the teacher did not handle other children the same way as she did me.

Don't get me wrong, she was nice and all of that, but the problem was that she felt 100% comfortable handling me the way she deemed valid, with no consultation from my parents.

This contrasted with making sure she communicated her intentions by asking permission of the parents of the other child in the class, who was also left-handed. Maybe it was a complete coincidence that the other child was not black, and for many, this may seem like a small and simple situation, but it wasn't. Not only was my learning stifled due to her inability to guide me, but I was also falling behind in my learning compared to other students in class by which was presented to be my own defects in intelligence. In fact, I ended up repeating first grade because of it. The system was subconsciously, systematically taking the first steps in changing my educational destiny negatively due to no failure of my own. Not having the same foundation as others established in something as simple as how to write had a major impact on my ability to grow skills for the next step in education. I won't play the complete victim and act as though my behavior didn't change in lieu of being behind because it did. I was embarrassed to not be on the same level as other students, and I acted out to express that distress. To this day, the system still misleads many students down a road of failure and despair behind implementations of unfair practices.

THE TALK

This is but one of my experiences in my educational journey, which is not to say they were all awful, as they were not. It is simply to shine a light on how much the use of power and privilege has an impact on individuals, in this case, as early as kindergarten.

Fast forwarding to high school, there were two educators that stood out to me as I look back at that time. I attended two high schools because of moving before graduating. The first school where I attended my freshman and sophomore years required a bus ride of about 45 minutes to travel to the location (integration and bussing at its finest) and, of course, 45 minutes back home. The second school I attended during my junior and senior years was in a different, larger city, where the location of the school was only a 10-minute commute from my home and provided a diverse student population.

The first educator that really impacted me was from my suburbia school with the 45-minute bus ride. He was a very nice math teacher; however, he was clear with me that, in his opinion, I did not possess the capacity to learn math and offered to move me to classes that he believed matched my ability. That ability was stated as REMEDIAL LEARNING. I believed him and accepted my lack of ability, as after all, he was an educational expert, right? Shortly thereafter, I started to give up on all academics that were not reading-based, and even those efforts were nowhere near my potential. He was so pleasant in his demeanor that I was sure he cared about my well-being and was being honest with me to protect me from embarrassment and disappointment.

The second educator was a gruff, tough old bird that taught psychology and chemistry at the second high school was 10 minutes from my home. He was very direct in his communication, which felt like he was insulting me most of the time. Looking back, I realize that I was simply not used to honest accountability in education. That made it easy for me to use as an excuse to take offense at everything he said. He often told me and others to do our work or get out of his class. I remember one day him telling me straight up that I didn't have the commitment it took to make it in a college chemistry class.

Conversations about the next steps in life and education were often at the center of all that he was teaching us. Hearing him tell me that I couldn't cut it in the next level of education didn't sit well with me at all.

How do you think things ultimately turned out under the tutelage of these two very different educators? Well... my first two years of high school were absolutely failures. Awful grades and awful memories. In fact, by the time I was done with the tenth grade, I was very serious about going to the Army so that I could be something in this life other than the direction I was going.

However, as a junior in high school, something changed. My last two years of high school turned into unbelievable improvements and positive experiences that shaped a large part of who I am today. It turns out that the second educator understood exactly what I was capable of and what I would need to be successful beyond high school. He pushed me, implemented accountability and used my rebellious nature against me, knowing that I would do anything to prove him wrong. He used his understanding and "privilege" to help me learn what was mandatory to be successful in academics. We ended up cultivating a great relationship, which was funny. An old white guy and a young, stubborn black kid coming from a rough educational start. I soon realized that the first educator really didn't care enough about me to put forth the effort to truly teach me. He very simply did what the system does most often: he cordially offered me failure with a smile. This often translates to welfare, jail or early death, with the caveat of "he just didn't have the ability to make it in society" as one gets older. The concept here is simple. Both men knew what I needed and what contributions it would take from them to help me advance in education, as this is supposed to be what teachers do for all students.

Only one teacher was willing to share the knowledge of his privilege with me. Privilege means his understanding of the educational system and how I could benefit from it if I applied myself and put in the work.

Learning the expectations of college organizations educationally, along with the discipline and accountability that were required to succeed within those confines, translated to what I needed for society. It changed my life, whether he meant to do so or not.

Privilege is such an interesting thing to me. At this point, it seems that people don't want to accept the fact that privilege automatically comes with power. That's just a reality of how any power structure, along with who controls it and who is included in it, works. Ultimately, just as no one can choose whether they are born black or white, you also cannot dictate whether you are born with or without privilege. What an individual chooses to do with the privilege they are born into is what is most important, in my opinion. It truly determines the color of the landscape around us. Using your position in life to succeed and provide benefit to others says so much more about what kind of human being you are, rather than a focus on how privileged you were. It's a tool, like anything else, that can be used selfishly or selflessly.

THE TALK

Although there are many situations I can reflect on from engaging with people who had privileges that I didn't have or couldn't understand at the time, these two teachers are prime examples of this concept early in life for me. I cannot stress how important it is to understand that POWER and PRIVILEGE go hand in hand. Like many other things in life, power and privilege do not have to be associated with a negative connotation if one chooses to do positive things with the gifts they are given.

With any type of privilege comes responsibility, whether we accept it or not. The ability to navigate through waters that aren't familiar to you can be difficult, regardless of one's status. Many people do not even realize that, as they are navigating through experiences, they are doing so with certain privileges. There is no one screaming on the sideline, "Hey! What you are doing is something that others cannot do!".

It has taken me many years to understand that many people don't know that the definition of what they see as everyday life for themselves can very much be a privilege to someone else. The responsibility everyone has comes into play once we are aware of what is happening and recognize what it means.

It's a similar concept to engaging with an American who has never visited a different country. That American probably has a definition of what inconvenience, hard times or problems are based on what they have experienced in this country. That individual may have no idea that potentially their worst day, worst experience or worst problem would be welcomed with open arms by someone in another country. The privilege of living in the United States is very real. This doesn't mean that there are no valid problems in this country that need attention, or that this American individual didn't experience hard times or bad days. It does mean that there are options we have access to and can take advantage of in this country simply because of the power structure we live in. Options that simply don't exist in other countries become perfect examples of "American privilege."

Being responsible with the gift of privilege also means we should not avoid conflict or bury our heads in the sand in hopes that challenges we know exist will just go away or only impact other people. One of the biggest examples of privilege avoidance I witness time and time again is when people use the phrase "I don't see color." That is one of the silliest comments I have heard. Of course, we all see color and every other physical characteristic of human beings. We see blonde hair, black hair, blue eyes, green eyes, skin tones, height, weight, big feet or small feet and more. We notice all these characteristics of people and more before a word is ever spoken, so why would anyone act as though they don't see color? Very simply stated.... AVOIDANCE.

If acting as though you don't see color means that you don't have to face the challenges that come along with acknowledging color, it makes perfect sense to say you don't see it? Or to say that it doesn't matter to you. It's a privilege that allows people to act as though they don't see color and continue with their day simply because THEY DON'T HAVE TO. When a person can move through a power structure and ignore a problem that's not impactful to them, the decision of avoidance comes into play. Do you avoid or engage? What are the consequences of those decisions? Can one lose their privilege by leaning into the issue or color and addressing the defects of the system? It's clearly not a comfortable topic to be involved in for any of us, especially when you don't know what perspective others have.

THE TALK

Years ago, I was on a plane to Vegas for a conference. I sat next to a middle-aged gentleman on what was a two-hour flight from our departure to our landing. Of course, in the beginning, the awkward silence and introductions took place before settling into normal conversation, as happens on most flights when sitting next to strangers. We talked about our professions and ended up landing on the topic of assumptions people often make about positions held in our professions. We were having a great conversation that seemed to be open, honest and direct. (Which I enjoy immensely on a regular basis, be it positive or negative) He suddenly hit me with, "It's too bad everyone can't treat each other better, I don't see color, I only see human beings." At this point, I felt like I was in a sitcom as I was looking right into the face of the camera with a blank stare. So…. again, if you don't already know this, please allow me to inform you. This is not a statement of solidarity or positivity to most people of color. IT IS NOT A GOOD THING TO SAY. It's very similar to cliché phrases such as "I'm not racist, I have black friends, there are black people in my family, I work with them at my job ", which these days sends the message that I AM RACIST AS HELL.

As risky as it may have been to engage in this kind of talk in such a closed space, I decided to go ahead and give my perspective to this gentleman with whom I had been having a great conversation. I shook my head and grinned slightly. I could tell in his eyes that he realized the direction I was going towards, or maybe his eyes saw the direction I wasn't going to go to. I asked him if, when he was searching for a partner for life, her physical appearance matter to him. He said, "Of course! It's not all about looks, but my type matters a lot." How about who you chose to represent your business? Does the appearance of that person matter? Again, he said, "Absolutely! If you don't have the right person representing your company, it can cause failure." I then asked, "Could you imagine a world where everyone looked exactly alike?" His reply was a resounding "NO!!! This life would be boring if everything and everyone were the same!" So then why in the world would you tell me that you don't see color? Can't you see where the insult in that statement is? Seeing all colors and qualities is an opportunity to recognize each individual person's greatness. When you don't see a person for who they are, you are, in essence, denying them the things that make them special. Diversity makes us all stronger, and we can't have that when the things that make us diverse are ignored. It comes across as an attempt to diminish the value of the attributes that make us all unique. He felt a bit embarrassed (I could tell), but he took my perception very well.

He had never thought about it like that because, quite frankly, he didn't have to. He honestly had never spoken to or listened to anyone of color about this subject. Yet here we were, two strangers talking about things that were probably avoided at home with those we worked with and saw every day. Engagement won over avoidance that day.

It's moments like this that remind me how much I love being a black man. I love being in a country that allows us to be free enough to have encounters like this. I wish it would happen more often positively. Most importantly, I love the opportunity to understand and be understood by those whose lives have been very different from mine. The give and take of learning from others and providing a different perspective to them feels to me like one of the vital parts of living. It is also true that not all encounters are always positive and do not always turn out as this situation did. However, sharing experiences and creating dialogue with those that have the power and privilege is an essential part of change.

THE TALK

"The opportunity to simply have conversations is vital to change." While this is not the only component of change, it is a substantial one. Very simply, I believe that "it takes power to change power. I am a firm believer that while others cannot fight your battles for you, one must have others in the fight with you to complete change. Some of the most cliché statements are also very true, such as "it takes a thief to catch a thief" or "only a soldier can stop a soldier," etc. When playing a game you did not create, you need allies who know how the game is played. People who believe in humanity and equality all need each other to change how this game has been played for so long. Without each other, we all fail.

Conversations, interactions and understanding between different walks of life are crucial to uniting humanity in power. It is important to recognize that there are many in the world who do not want these kinds of alliances to take place.

"Power" itself doesn't see color; it sees control of everything under it. That means every color in humanity. True economic power in numbers is simple when you look at who has wealth and who does not. Only 10% of the U.S. population has a household income of 200k or more. That's about 33 million. Well, the truth is that there are only 46 million black people in this country, which has 329 million. If you subtract the 33 million making 200k or more, that still leaves 296 million people who have nowhere near the same economic power as that 10%. Newsflash and math flash, that 296 million left over are not only black people that don't have true economic power.

The most dangerous power play in this country is the one where the 'have-nots' come together to hold the 'haves' accountable for fairness and equality. The have-nots represent all races, creeds and colors as we are all in the same boat.

"Have-nots" don't just fall into the category of people below the poverty line. It's more so a defining statement of those who are not wielding the same power as those in the household; incomes find fantastic tax breaks in their favor. The have-nots are brainwashed to believe we are not all in the same financial boat, but really, we are. As a result, we don't have conversations about the truth or about what's really going on in our society and why. There are times, some people who have power or the "haves" do try to help to make things better for society by showing us what's behind the power curtain, and many of us still refuse to engage.

We tell ourselves, "That situation doesn't apply to me," and we continue with our heads in the sand. Many of us do not acknowledge our self-worth and lash out at others as a distraction from holding ourselves accountable. As "have-nots", we rarely hold the line on anything substantial and waste time finding someone to blame to make ourselves feel better, rather than being part of a solution. Just to be clear again, the have-nots I am speaking about consist of whites, blacks, Latinos and everyone else. We then wonder why communities cannot implement consistent change when awful things happen in our society. We wonder why politicians have a foothold on policies most of us are not in favor of. We refuse to look at ourselves to step up and implement change.

Revolutions can be sparked by one single situation when the opportunity is seized, but true change doesn't happen without the unification of all who share a common goal, regardless of the individual reasons why that goal was selected.

FEAR/ EDUCATION/ POVERTY/ LAW = THE TOOLS OF POWER

"If you can convince the lowest white man he's better than the best colored man, he won't notice you're picking his pocket. Hell, give him somebody to look down on and he'll empty his pockets for you."

Lyndon B Johnson.

"If you want to hide something from the negro, hide it in a book."

Carter G Woodson.

Hell of a way to start a dialogue, right? Just come out smacking both white and black folks all upside the head.... In the process of digesting these quotes, it seemed to me that these kinds of statements are often received as something directed at a person and not to a person. The last thing I want is for any of this to seem like pieces of information being shoved at you rather than being offered to you. Moving forward, this dialogue is all about us having a conversation as I did and still do face-to-face with my 76-year-old counterpart, people in my past, or those that I trade perspectives with on social media. This talk will use facts, real-life experiences, and perspectives in our conversations. The difference, of course, is that you are reading this versus speaking to me live and directly.

It reminds me of the same way my mother first sat me down about how to handle interactions with police and try not to die. Much like those conversations that were presented to me by her, this will mirror that same exchange in presentation to you. The "exchange" I will have with you will be rooted in a conversation about you and me in America. If I am to be honest, this is also about me continuing to learn and evolve regarding present and past experiences engaging with people of all demographics. I have already discovered some new things about myself in the early stages of this conversation. So, let's keep it simple and straight while we take this short journey together.

Now that we have that out of the way, we should talk about the two quotes above. For me, these are two very impactful quotes that could be considered extremely offensive yet true at the same time. Which reminds me that truth is often offensive; however, one should not shy away from something honest just because it stings. Both of these quotes embrace the tools of fear, lack of education and the system of poverty to manipulate the intended audience into the position those in power want you to stay in.

One of the scariest things about these TOOLS is that they are nothing new. The same tools have been used since the beginning of time by those in power and still work on the masses to this day. Yes, I call them tools because that's exactly what they are, and they are used to get an outcome, just as a shovel is used to dig a hole. What's worse, most of us simply refuse to see what is happening and choose to live in denial. That denial is often fueled by things such as fear of anything different, change, lack of education, misinformation, diminished resources, and the lack of revenue or equity, better known as POVERTY.

It's kind of unbelievable that Lyndon Johnson would say this quote out loud like this, isn't it? You would think this could cause all kinds of problems for those in power, but it didn't. Why do you suppose that is? I think that fear and poverty have been stronger tools used against the public at large than our own drive and self-motivation have been.

The fear of anything different from us, fear of self-reflection, fear of competition, fear of accountability, inferiority complexes, fear of retribution to those mistreated and ultimately fear of a truth that is not in your favor are concepts that apply to us all.

Those in power know that fear is one of the biggest opponents of success. Fear is also one of the best separators and segregators known to man. Actions and reactions due to fear have isolated and murdered more people historically than can be counted.

All of this sounds strong in theory, but what does this really mean in a practical sense? I have some examples that are relevant specifically to this quote about the white men that President Johnson was talking about.

Not to say that there are not examples of fear that are very much applicable to the black man and how he moves in this space, because there are. However, this quote was specific to white people spoken by a white person in a very powerful position.

These are some of the fears that the public was programmed to believe by those in power that engulf the white community to this day.

From my early years as a 10-year-old black male child to as recent as a week ago (we don't need to disclose my current age).

White people would double-lock their car doors when I walked by. I don't think you understand me.... the car door is already locked, but they see me and lock it again. All you could hear was the hard click of the lock snapping.

It doesn't matter if I am in a full suit or jogging pants, the fear of me is the same. I have experienced it for decades. I just laugh now, although it's really not funny, but we often laugh so we don't cry. Especially in my own neighborhood, currently, where houses range from a quarter million dollars up to 1.8 million. The crazy part is that these folks (not all, but some) are genuinely afraid of me like the boogie man. Where do you suppose that comes from? Why do people feel this way? What has fueled these fears? Is there overwhelming crime in affluent areas with black people terrorizing and brutalizing white people? If that were the case, do you think well-to-do neighborhoods would still be thriving generations later? Probably not. (Most informed people know that the majority of crimes are driven by proximity, not stereotypes.) Black people have the unfortunate legacy of historical misrepresentation and the perpetuation of heinous stereotypes for generations. News and television have been among the greatest propagators of fear historically. For generations, the only roles on the media screen black people could assume were those of slaves, janitors, criminal thieves, murderers and rapists who would come to get your daughters. Imagine someone who had never met or seen someone black in person leveraging their entire perspective from cinematic imagery?

Is it any wonder that before even speaking to me, so many white people are terrified?

It's no longer a surprise to me when someone talks to me and says, "Oh my gosh, you are so well spoken." They don't even realize how offensive that is when they say it, nor do they realize that they just admitted that the fear of stereotypes has a full grip on them. Of course, I am well spoken, why the hell wouldn't I be? If you are, why can't I be as well? Those in power have done an amazing job giving white people someone to simultaneously fear and look down on through fictitious imagery.

Have you ever noticed that when a person of color commits a crime, their picture and background history are immediately on trial and displayed for all to see? These days, even videos of black people being wrongly abused or killed are preceded by showing if the victim ever committed a crime in their life, as if that is relevant to being shot to death over a routine traffic stop, ID check or walking through a neighborhood where someone reported a suspicious person. SURPRISE… to a certain extent, it's been like that since news broadcasts began.

My grandmother could tell me when I was a kid back in the 70s if a crime was committed by a white person or a black person within 2 minutes of the story coming on the news. Very simply, she would say that someone killed someone, but they aren't saying a name or showing a face, which was the indicator to her that the criminal was white. To this day, I can gauge the news the same way 90% of the time.

This type of manipulation is another fear tactic to make people believe that **blacks commit more crimes than anyone else**, and it clearly continues to work. The FBI's yearly stats say otherwise, though. In my opinion, manipulation of data through false media and perpetuation of reality degradation TV have been the most successful assault on the WHITE communities' intelligence and stoking of hate and fear. Yes, I said assaults on the white community because they are being manipulated and victimized on a level as well. Even though information like the FBI stats and government data is available for all to find, those in power have convinced the white community that black/Latino people use up all the welfare dollars, Spanish-speaking people take all the jobs, and come in through open borders to be the secondary criminals of the country. ("keep America first"). We are told that those two groups commit all of the crimes and get all of the favorable treatments in gaining asylum, education opportunities and work due to affirmative action. I still can't understand how, in the same breath, politicians can say that immigrants are taking American jobs but are also costing taxpayers' money from them using government assistance, while being nothing but criminals.

When I tell people about the actual crime and social data, they are often shocked beyond words. Speaking to a colleague a few years ago about welfare, I showed him the data that 30% of whites were on welfare, which was not shocking until he saw that at that time, 30% of 298 million white people was roughly 89 million whites on welfare. There were only 45 million black people in the whole country then. Of those 45 million black people, about 17 million were using the welfare system in some capacity. Yes, it's a higher percentage based on our population, but blacks are not the number that is strapping the system down. Yet, whites vote against welfare programs as they are being led to believe this is how you stop black people from negatively impacting the economy. They don't realize they are really voting to punish more white people than any other group of people. Hell of a fear from manipulation that causes others to cut off their own nose to spite their face, as instructed by those in power.

The same manipulation has been done with crime data, job data and "favorable" treatment beliefs. Years ago, I was in Kentucky engaging in a debate around black people getting opportunities just because they are black and not due to the skill levels they have. The gentleman believed it was reverse discrimination and unfair. As I began to quote educational and social institutions that for GENERATIONS historically wouldn't hire me, but also wouldn't allow me (black people) into the institutions other than as a janitor, he began to realize that without certain legal changes, there would never be any diversity in the here and now unless organizations were made to change by law. I also pointed out that if he himself didn't fit the mold of that good ole boy network, he wouldn't get into those institutions either for work or social purposes.

You know…like the country clubs that didn't allow any people of color to belong to them, and only certain white families with certain connections could be members. The more we talked, the more the point began to hit home for the gentleman. It wasn't just about people like me; it was also about people like him, who were not in power; he had just been fooled.

In reflecting back over the last ten years of my life, a big impact I noticed regarding whites and blacks in the media had to be reality TV. It was the perfect platform to invoke the public's fears, judgment and joy of someone else's misery and misfortune, all while enforcing stereotypes of a few as the reality of many.

The stereotypical, misogynistic clichés of all races were well represented. How many of us enjoyed tuning in to see who would be "fired" in next week's episode or who would be kicked off the island or betrayed by someone they trusted? How about those looking to see who provoked a fight or reacted in physical violence, which allowed us to say, "See, that's the problem with those people, even with money and success, they are still savages."

THE TALK

It's an amazing concept when you take a step back and recognize the power of entertainment and the media. Quite frankly, it has been that way for generations, and we as the American people still buy into the myths we are fed by these entities lock, stock and barrel. Reality TV, in my opinion, ushered in the next level of misinformation being accepted.

The fears that tools like this can instill in people's minds have no bounds.

I can't tell you how many encounters I have witnessed where individuals are terrified of situations simply because of what they have seen on television. Fears of how dangerous, violent and angry all black men are perceived to be. Even with today's technology, if all you know about a group of people different from you is the images portrayed on a screen, how detrimental can that be? If those images are not positive or at least balanced, it will impact your perception of how they may be when a face-to-face encounter happens. It's bad enough that human beings already naturally fear what they don't understand and what is different from their own norms.

It sucks when people fear that I will rob or kill them, no matter how I look or the actions that I take. The thought that I exist in skin that most are afraid of daily is exhausting. The battle against fear is age-old and never-ending.

The most ironic thing to me is that the best tool against fear is one that this country seems to put less focus on year after year.... Education. On a very basic level, I know that education annihilates fear through example and experience, as I have lived it time and time again. One of the strongest motivations I had in creating this project was based on using education and dilute the fears others had about me and people like me. Being able to talk with someone and break down barriers of stereotypes and false narratives with data and real-life examples has shown the power of education time and time again. (you know that whole content of character thing) People who fear you typically do not know you, nor do they expect you to have intelligence of the institutional kind or the viable life lesson kind.

In my neck of the woods, we would say that is having both "book smarts" and a "street degree." Imagine the surprise when they see that you have both types of intelligence and realize the media images about you were wrong?

Though I did not actually graduate from college, I am very aware of how important it is to carry both types of intelligence, no matter what background you come from. Earlier, I described some of my experiences with teachers I encountered in the younger years of my life, but allow me to clarify, I was not heavily invested in learning. Quite frankly, school would have been completely avoided if I thought I could have gotten away with not going. It wasn't until I was older that I truly valued learning and how much of an equalizer education was in all facets of life.

This quote below was told to me when I was younger by a man who was much older but had a lot of experience and understanding in both worlds of intelligence.

"The most dangerous black men in this country are not the educated businessmen or the men with street credit; it's the black men who have both of these dynamics that are the most feared."

Education in the traditional sense provides the framework to understand how to operate in a system that has rules that the neighborhood you come from may not understand. Education bridges gaps between you and others, providing compatibility where before there may have been none. Education allows one to understand how a system is designed to work, how it physically works, and if the system is productive. (By System, I mean the institutions that run this country) I once asked an older acquaintance of mine who was not black if she was shocked when she engaged in conversations with educated black people. Not only did she state that she was shocked, but each time this occurred, she was pleasantly surprised. She stated she felt guilty that she was surprised and how wrong her perceptions had been. The realization that one has fallen victim to believing stereotypes can also be a hard pill for any of us to swallow.

If education can be such an equalizer, why is it not a priority for more black people to attain it and use it? You would think that obtaining an education would simply be a given and an easy way to remove more of the barriers for not just black people, but everyone. But it is not. Why do you think things are this way?

While I won't pretend to act as though I have answers for white people, I do have some thoughts about black folks' education and why. There are deep-rooted barriers when it comes to access to many things with black people in this country. Education is one of the biggest barriers. While these barriers are factual, I only have theories about their impacts on them if I am to be honest. One of the factual barriers is very simply that it was illegal for black people to read or write in this country for far too many generations. As we all know, most educational institutions in this country did not allow black people to attend them for generations. The impact of this deprivation has been a monumental setback in the competitive education of the black community. Yet society still acts as though this is fiction, not fact.

The historic impact the deprivation of education created also perpetuated the negative outlook white people cast towards black people from slavery to date is earth-shaking. To this day, many white individuals are still blown away when engaging with a black person who regurgitates intelligent candor. How do I know? Because the phrase "you speak so well" is still the first thing to come out of the mouths of people that I engage with. To be honest, I can't tell you how many emails I have written that have garnered the reply, "Wow! That was really well written," as opposed to just addressing the subject matter of the document. You might ask why I wouldn't just take the compliment and move on. I would say that these are not the kinds of compliments you give to everyday individuals in business. The compliments you give to the normal businessperson are praise for the content, problem-solving solving and execution of his or her dialogue or written text, not the ability to put together a comprehensive sentence. That is a demeaning response, whether the person on the other end recognizes it or not. Is this a reaction because the public at large recognizes how long education was legally prohibited for people like me? Or is this a response under the perception that people like me are inferior, with no regard to the restrictions of the past? You tell me?

Speaking of demeaning, I must change gears for a moment and bring you up to speed on an encounter I just faced. While the situation is nowhere near new to me, at this point, I simply had to sit down and document this to get it off my chest and not explode.

Let's call this situation "My Day."

"On the night before my birthday, 8/29/2020, I read that Chadwick Boseman passed away due to colon cancer that no one knew about publicly. This man, who embodied characters on the big screen such as Jackie Robinson, Thurgood Marshall, James Brown and Marvel comics 'Black Panther, had become an iconic inspiration to millions of people marginalized and liberated. His talent allowed many people of color to see themselves on the screen in ways hardly ever portrayed as royalty and incredible examples of beautiful, talented, smart human beings. You know, the way a lot of us really are.

The next morning, I turned 50 years old during a pandemic, civil unrest unlike anything this country has seen since the 60s, one of the most polarizing election years ever and another devastating hurricane (Laura) that hit Louisiana the day before, as if it's not enough that my birthday also marks the anniversary of Hurricane Katrina.

Regardless of all these crazy things going on, I decided to get up early, throw on my Marvel T-shirt and put in 3 miles with my Labrador retriever to ease my mind. About a mile and a half into the morning, a vehicle pulls up alongside me with an older couple inside. They say "good morning! "And I respond back with a smile. The gentleman looks in my eyes, points at my shirt and says, "Didn't I read about you last night in the news?" and began to chuckle. The implication was very simply about Mr. Boseman, meaning he was I and I am him, but now he is dead. As a black man in America, your ability to read between the lines is cultivated at an early age. It was all that I could do not to let the piercing look on my face manifest into the physical action of my body. I simply kept going."

Some would say that this is a small thing in the grand scheme of things, but to laugh at and tear down a person's role models, heroes, or positive examples that they have been deprived of for generations is unacceptable. Remember how sensitive everyone was to the death of JFK and how people felt when Malcom X made comments about him? This truly speaks to one of the many reasons so many have taken to the streets and, in some cases, yes, become violent. How many generations of poking someone in the eye while terrorizing them can be sustained before they lose it?

Don't talk to me about law and order or abiding by rules when it's never been fair and equal for all people. Let's not forget that this is the same country that said it was legal to own, sell, rape, torture and murder me as your property. Stop me from voting, using your bathrooms, restaurants, and country clubs. It was illegal for me to speak up for myself, engage in conversations with certain people and illegal for me to read...... ILLEGAL FOR ME TO READ. People just like me historically were KILLED legally for things like this and much more.

So, the next time you speak of law and order, remember how an unjust system punishes certain people, while simultaneously condemning others when they stand up for what should be fair and lawful justice...... aggressively.... by any means necessary.

It was a hell of a beginning to an already challenging day. But like many people in this country, you find a way to calm your spirit and press on.

OKAY!!!!! Now that I got that out of my system, let's continue with where we were, shall we? EDUCATION, the deprivation and, in some cases to date, the rejection of it by so many people of color. The ridicule that came with using one's intelligence and obtaining an education began to spread in the black community over time. Before we knew it, we began attacking each other the same as society attacked us for trying to be better. Perhaps this is because so few in our communities really had the opportunity to excel in education, while many more were just left behind. It became normal to be labeled things like "Joe College," preppy boy, or someone who wanted to be "white" if you did well in school or got the chance to continue higher education. Black people had been brainwashed into believing that being smart was more of an attribute of being white or being well-versed in white culture. Being black carried implications that you were automatically ignorant, uneducated and only cut out for crime, sports or the lesser career positions in life? It becomes much easier to embrace that you are nothing in life when a country expects you to be nothing or takes everything from you every time you become more than nothing. The strength it takes to negate the mindset of the masses and fight to embrace that you are an amazing individual with talents and characteristics the world wishes it had naturally is something many cannot understand. Most importantly, it is hard to remember in tough situations that you and people like you have suffered... you... are... still...here.

The stigma that education doesn't belong to us is one that we embraced much more than the forefathers thought we would when it was denied to us. Unfortunately, history books in this country were not written to fairly reflect the true society of black people who were shipped here came from. The intelligence, innovation, culture, fashion and essence of life that have contributed to the endurance of a land that wasn't ours were never honored as they should be. As a result, we reject being the Kings and Queens we are based on where we come from. It has been proven that if you can take away a person's history, you can change the essence of who they are. There is a saying that has been around since slavery "ended" that goes something like this, "If you want to hide something from a black man, just put it in a book." What's crazy about this phrase to me is how many of us jumped on the bandwagon using this against each other. We engage as if we really believe the problem with black people and education is around being lazy and unmotivated to achieve it as the root cause. Information has been in books much longer than the time of the established United States of America. The reason it was illegal for us to learn to read here was so that we could be mentally oppressed by those who were in power. The phrase "If you want to keep something from a black person, hide it in a book" at one point in time literally meant that if black people found that information and stated it verbally, they could be killed simply for reading.

One of the most fascinating conversations I previously had was with a few of my older children a couple of years ago regarding history and those in power. Being that old school dad who is always pushing how to grow and be better with career, education and awareness, the conversation about phones came up. Entertainment use vs education use. "Why does it have to be one or the other? Why not both? We can be entertained while acknowledging the use of this built-in encyclopedia, a research giant we hold in our hands?" I told them that all the questions and curiosities they usually have can be answered with your phone. Searching multiple sources, confirming numbers, data and research through viable platforms can provide you with insane knowledge of your history, where you come from and how to avoid repeating negative history. I then explained that the point of using this tool revolves around understanding the engagement of power. Vanity is a direct result of power. Those in power must celebrate and document all that they do to win. This means from the most heinous acts committed to the heroic gestures used to define who they claim to be. Throughout history, almost all actions that have transpired by those at the top have always been documented. The people should never be led astray or misinformed about the truth, because the answers are almost always literally at our fingertips. Those in power know that entertainment and distraction are more appealing than seeking out the truth that exists. Therefore, there is no fear in documenting how one becomes and maintains "the master of his universe." What's most amazing to me is the fact that all of us have a choice to type and search for the truth or scroll to be entertained by the lie. You know which one wins the most, don't you? This is what I showed my children so that if nothing else, they are cognizant of it. I wanted my kids to understand why suppressing education has been a grassroots effort to support oppression for 500 years in our country.

What those in power understood was that physical oppression only lasts so long before those who are oppressed revolt against you. Mother Nature makes the rules in the survival of the fittest realm, and she creates the strongest; mankind does not. However, mental oppression can be used to keep one group of people oppressed and another in power for generations. The tools of mental oppression that those in power utilize are things such as Liquor stores on every corner in certain communities, funneling support for drugs to thrive in specific areas and fast-food restaurants in abundance that destroy the health of a group's bodies. Exposure to sub-par housing and living conditions, economic redlining depressing the market value of where one lives, Jim Crow laws limiting freedoms, theft of a group's innovations, low-quality schools, intimidation in over policing, sub-par hospital care and nonexistent infrastructure, all perpetuated by minimal financial resources. The blueprint of POVERTY.

Before I go on what many might call a tangent, let me be clear about a few things. Poverty does not only impact black people. All of the "tools" mentioned beforehand, integrated by those in power, can be applied in any low-income area regardless of race. AGAIN....POVERTY DOES NOT ONLY IMPACT BLACK PEOPLE OR PEOPLE OF COLOR. The most important thing that poverty does is maintain the space in between the HAVES and the HAVE-NOTS. Newsflash, there are more HAVE NOTS that are white in this country than there are that are black! This has always been the true root cause of everything. Please do not be confused; understand that economics is at the top of it all. Racism, injustice, misogynistic behavior, chauvinism, ageism and on and on are all simply the tools that those at the top of the economic food chain use to keep the rest of us distracted at each other's throats as while they keep their hands in all of our pockets.

Having said that, one must know that poverty serves as a most valuable marketing tool for those in power than anything other concept. For example, every race has its poverty levels in a society; however, ask yourself what is showcased, or I should say who is showcased? What do you see more than anything? How many commercials have you seen to help a poor African child in poverty? A lot, right? Now, how many commercials have you seen to help a freezing white child in Europe or the tundra of Russia? How about Ireland's impoverished communities that have next to nothing to eat? The homeless problems in France or Italy? How about a commercial to sponsor a poor white kid in England starving? How is Tiny Tim these days? Hmmmm.... you haven't seen that? Ok, how about the low-income white population in this country? Surely that makes it onto television so that we can help them, right? Let me guess, only the trailer park white individuals are the ones in need, and there aren't that many?

As I stated before, there are about *90 million white Americans* utilizing food stamps and housing aid in this country on average, each year. (THAT'S GOVERNMENT ASSISTANCE IN CASE YOU DIDN'T CATCH THAT)

There are about 16-18 million black people using the same welfare benefits as well. There are some people reading this in shock right now because they are certain that those numbers are wrong and should be reversed. There are millions of people thinking about how all we hear and see are people of color being lazy, not getting a job and living off the "working man's" tax dollars. Well.... the truth is, there are about 45 million black people in the country and about 298 million white or "other" people in the country. We have all been consistently lied to about who uses social services the most in this country. Furthermore, when people vote to disband those services, they do so because they believe it's blacks, Latinos and illegal immigrants utilizing them in the majority, which is also not correct. Another trick/tactic of those in power.

People do not know that they are really shooting their own groups in the foot and cutting program dollars just to line the pockets of special interest government groups, but the local politicians have folks believing publicized lies. Again, remember Lyndon B Johnson. He told you what those in power were doing to not only people of color, but to white people as well.

You see... when the powers that be pick and choose what the face of poverty looks like, they can manipulate everyone into feeling like no matter how bad things get,

at least I am not THAT face of poverty. When really, the truth is the opposite.

It's all our faces.

It just doesn't look like what they show us all on the news, on television shows and in the movies, but yes, it sure is the opposite of what we are shown. You know what amazes me the most? All that anyone has to do is go and look up the true data of what is going on, and they will see how much the everyday black and white person is being pimped by the system. ANYONE CAN FIND THIS INFORMATION!! Instead, we think we can pick a winning side (Democrat or Republican), join in on the lies both parties tell and be a part of the winners.

The true winners would emerge if folks believed in the phrase "we the people" and stood up for what was right and wrong. If we advocated for things fair and just, it would make those who think they are in power realize that we are actually the ones with power. Unfortunately, racial tension and poverty are the tools/distractions used to keep us at each other's throats.

Think of it in these terms... imagine being on the sinking Titanic and fighting with 20 people in the flooding ballroom. While you are fighting about a spot you want, two people on the other side of the ship are getting on the last lifeboat, which has 20 open spaces on it. The lifeboat deploys with 18 open seats. How crazy is that? Do you believe that you would engage in something so ridiculous as that? Well… in most cases, the overwhelming answer is and has been yes. You see, this scenario is at parity with what MOST Americans do in this country every single, damn day. We fight over things among each other that are unimportant, while a minority of people benefit from the distractions we all get lost in. Those people live and prosper, while "we the people" drown.

Another example of systemic poverty that comes to mind is one that was still active up until the early 1970s. In certain parts of the country, when applying for government assistance, individuals had to state how many persons, and their ages, were living in the household. For Black families, when the patriarch was listed in the paperwork, the family was told they didn't qualify for assistance. As soon as the patriarch was not on the paperwork, approval was granted. Not only did the father have to be absent from paperwork, but some cities would conduct "midnight raids" (or inspections, as they termed it) to see if a black man was in the house. If there were, the family would lose benefits automatically. Of course, that turned the family against the father figure of the household and often meant he needed to leave so that benefits could be received. This later became another sensationalized arm of the attack: "black men don't take care of their families; they are not in the home." On the other side of the coin, those were not the same requirements when it came to many white families filling out the exact same paperwork for assistance, which meant that the white male never had to go anywhere to get additional support from the government when falling on challenging times. The white male could actually benefit from the government support and rise out of a low economic situation. Keep in mind, the first welfare systems began in the 1930s with individual states and then in 1935 with the federal government.

The perpetuation of the black father abandoning the household has been the mantra since men were sold and split from their families in the early 1600s here. Since that era, the mantra has evolved either by switching to incarcerating black men by the thousands, sending black men to war disproportionately via the draft to die, manufacturing easier access to drug use and addiction in communities rather than education and opportunity, public emasculation of the black male and so on.

Systemic oppression has given way to many modes of segregation, like the special codes that would be put on loan applications for mortgages that would flag loan officers to either reject the loan or approve it with inflated interest rates for people of color. The average everyday citizen had no idea that this kind of thing was happening. When it would be exposed, it would then be portrayed in the news as something else, such as a one-off mistake or a hoax that everyone would believe and buy into. As we all know, if you label anything the same way long enough, perception very much becomes reality.

As long as I can remember, I have been surrounded by individuals who realized that if the playing field were truly level, they also would have been wealthy professional contributors to society. Because things have never been level or fair, most individuals ended up taking what they were allowed to have humbly and not causing problems for their family. Sure, every so often, someone gets to break out of the normal role, but that is not the norm. The majority is always told to be like the few that attain monumental success, when we all know why the odds are stacked against that. Both of my grandfathers should have been millionaires based on intelligence, work ethic and talent alone. One grandparent retired from a well-known Auto Company after 30-plus years, which alone should have changed his life, but on top of that, he was also a golf expert and should have been a pro. He was only allowed to caddy at the country club where he was better than all the members who played there. My other grandfather was a high school educator and a veteran who easily could have been a professor at a major university, but settled for a good life as a colored" teacher in the face of the civil rights battles. I understood that both knew rocking the boat could cost them and the ones they loved their lives in the era they lived in. So, I was very careful, even as a child, never to question or chastise as to why they didn't "do more" with their lives. At a young age, I knew that they had truly made the ultimate sacrifice.

Poverty and the fears of living in it have been used to keep people in line for generations, and for some reason, the majority of people in all walks of life in this country just accept it. I suppose groups feel that it's easier to keep fighting with those whom you believe are beneath you than to go against those standing over you, lowering the ceiling of opportunity. Many of us, unfortunately, seem to displace energy towards the wrong people and direction.

Growing up, I remember how desperate many were to escape the shadow or even perception of poverty in any way they could. If it meant buying a car you probably couldn't afford, dressing in clothes that were outside of the budget they had, or acting as though your bank account was bigger than it was, that's what would happen. The name of the game was "fake it even if you never really make it". As long as things looked like they were better for you, they really were. Trying to establish an image or a reputation was more important than anything else simply because the chance of ever genuinely being able to claim true success status was highly unlikely. Sounds like modern-day Facebook, doesn't it? Create an image that people like and follow regardless of its validity.

Many chose to work outside of the system acceptable by law, which brought a lot of flash and instant success. As my grandfather always said, "One way or another, a man is going to work." He was right about that. Unfortunately, some of that "work" many did resulted in death or incarceration while losing everything that really matters. If we are truly honest about the landscape, how can anyone really knock individuals taking all options available when the doors of acceptable opportunity are literally slammed closed in their faces? Especially when the doors are closed by the so-called powers that be. In fact, those same powers have often provided the under-the-table resources that create revenue for the individuals who engage in the kind of work that is deemed unacceptable and illegal. The catch.... The authorities get a piece of the money one is making illegally (the biggest piece at that), and the individual can be discarded at any time the objective is achieved, or the individual's value is no longer viable. Let's be clear, I am not making excuses for anyone doing wrong or justifying negative behavior. However, to act as though systemic influence and lack of opportunity do not impact the choices human beings make is ostrich-like thinking and irresponsible rationale.

Have any of you ever been hungry before? I mean, REALLY hungry, like no substantial food for days. Well... when you are hungry, what do you think happens when someone sits you down in front of a buffet? Do you put your napkin in your lap and carefully select a meat to cut with your knife into pieces and consume? Or do you grab any and everything in sight, stuffing yourself to the point that you get sick, not chewing the food, consuming as fast as possible before it is taken away?

This same comparison is what happens when a person or group of people is deprived of or has never had money or material things. You can never get enough. Once it begins, you feel you can't acquire enough, and most of all, you often cannot see any pitfalls coming while you are blinded by the need to fill that "have-not" void. This premise is at the root of why, in low economic areas, individuals engage in acts that get themselves or others killed or jailed.

What is most amazing about those who seek to fill this void by working under circumstances that are considered 'illegal' is not the actual crimes engaged in, but the fact that the appearance of the individual becomes the determining factor of whether a crime may or may not actually be seen as criminal, especially when it comes to the drug and money game. Who you are and where you do it make an enormous difference. Why is that? That, my friends, is indeed the question. That brings us to LAW and the foundation of what it is, how it works and who it applies to in our country.

One of the best examples of modern-day law hypocrisy that is mind-blowing would be comparing the mid-80s and the crack cocaine epidemic to the last three years (2020,2019, and 2018) onslaught of the opioid epidemic.

What would you say if I described the following: A drug exists that impacts men, women and children by causing almost instant addiction, driving the user to do anything to gain the means to purchase the drug. Its euphoric effects are temporary, which means the need to reproduce that original feeling creates the demand to find money by any means necessary for purchases 24 hours a day. Selling stolen merchandise, stealing, prostitution, assault, violent crimes, and betraying loved ones were among the lengths the user would resort to. Use of the drug results in mental illness, brain damage, suicides, depression, malnutrition and a wide array of diseases transmitted via sexually contact, as well as the destruction of internal organs resulting in multiple forms of death.

This is not the opioid crisis I am describing.... This is the crack epidemic that impacted two generations of not solely, but primarily, minority populations in the United States. During this epidemic, one would think that the same measures that were taken to battle it would have been implemented equally towards the opioid crisis, correct? Offering treatments and humane ways to help those recover from an addiction problem that has gripped their lives. Incarceration is no place for a suffering addict to get help, and rehabilitate is the mantra for opioid addicts. Brutalizing and killing addicts won't help the problem, right? That is not what happened when it wasn't opioids.

The entire volume of all law books and then some were thrown at the crack epidemic. Addicts had crack babies in jail, many were left to die on the streets as informants with no medical care provided. Arrests were through the roof, along with sentence minimums that made no sense for those who are addicts and in trouble. The legal system had no mercy on the victims of crack or the impact it had on their families and communities. This may convince some folks that I do not have sympathy for those caught up in the opioid problem right now; however, that is nowhere near true. What is true is that the same considerations for those minority communities who suffered a similar fate with an addictive drug did not exist from the mid-80s up through 2012.

Opioid addiction, interestingly enough, does not have anywhere near the rate of minority victims as crack cocaine did. By victims, I don't just mean users or dealers; I mean those impacted by it. That applies to families, streets, neighborhoods, hell, entire communities across the country. America didn't seem to implement the same response when young white males and females began showing up in hospitals, homeless shelters, and suicidal, betraying families for money, committing crimes and losing their lives to opioids as they did when crack did that to minorities. So, the laws changed, incarcerations changed, rehabilitation changed, and empathy changed.

That was an extremely long comparison, just too simply to say that the laws for one group of people are not the same as the laws for another group, wasn't it? One of the conversations that I have had with my children is explaining why people of color in the country feel like they do about law enforcement. This example of drug addiction is, in actuality, a small one, comparatively speaking, but a very valid one indeed.

The foundations of fear and distrust of law enforcement are quite simple.

It begins in the late 1600s, early 1700s, with Slave patrols. These were groups of men original tasked with retrieving or dealing with difficult or defiant slaves. They were the ones who would chase down these slaves with the legal authority to bring them back or kill them if returning them was not possible. These slave patrols evolved over decades as law enforcement over people of color to keep them in line and, more importantly, enslaved. Militias were also enlisted as groups responsible for tracking down and recovering those who had escaped. In the short term, law enforcement officers for white citizens would also be slave patrollers. Which means the laws they would enforce on white citizens were starkly different from what was enforced on slaves. From the beginning, there were two sets of laws for two groups of people. It was not against the law to brutalize, abuse and murder black people. Black people had no rights, were not seen as citizens and were not a part of the governing laws that had been established by the constitution or the legal system. In essence, laws were made to ensure minorities followed them and fell in line.

The Emancipation Proclamation, which freed slaves, actually became an obstacle for slave patrollers; therefore, an adjustment was made. It was put into law that if you were arrested for committing a crime, you could be convicted of a felony and put back into servitude (slavery). Suddenly, black people were the culprits of committing the majority of crimes in America, and slave patrollers were back in business, rounding up minorities for courts all over that would convict them and place them back in slavery.

In a nutshell, this is the history of law enforcement's disposition towards minorities, with a caveat of why many of the traits and behaviors by officers today are traceable back to the barbarism of slave patrols back then. Though the actual slave patrols ended after the Civil War, the tactics they used became the blueprint for policing black communities as history moved along. Much like now, infiltration of the Ku Klux Klan and supremacist members into law enforcement agencies elevated and perpetuated said brutality.

These are the kinds of behaviors and tactics that most white citizens have never experienced and, in many cases, truly do not even know exist. It's quite frankly one of the reasons so many white Americans were shocked and appalled by the public murder of George Floyd. Meanwhile, many people of color were not shocked by seeing this at all and simply wondered why it took so long for the rest of you to understand that this has been the norm for generations. Strange way to look at things, right?

Just for the record, this is not to say that all law enforcement officers are murdering white supremacists or that white people who didn't realize what was happening are complicit and should feel guilty. This, unfortunately, is just stating what has happened. Yes, people will feel some kind of way about this, but being defensive and deflective solves absolutely nothing. Truth can be painful, but it is also the path to change and growth.

The interesting thing about laws in our country is the hypocrisy of them. As a society, we lean on the rule of law to be the right thing to do; however, we never acknowledge the flaws in the rule of law or the flaws in the systems that create laws. So often you will hear someone say, Just comply, obey the law, and you will be fine. We tend to forget things like it was once against the law for: black people to read/ woman to vote, black people to vote, black people to use a white bathroom, interracial dating and marriage, entrance into the front door of a white store if you were black, attend universities, enter country clubs, dine in restaurants, live in certain neighborhoods, own certain property and even be in certain parts of town. So... if the law can be so flawed and unjust, can anyone say that if you just comply, follow the law, and all will be okay? Well, it all depends on who you are as to whether you will be okay or not. For folks who look like me, it will not be okay, and most likely, I will not make it home alive. To be direct about it, sometimes laws that have been created were inhumane and simply wrong. History shows that, not me.

Again, this is not to say that any group of people should be able to do whatever they like and not follow any type of order or protocol. It is to say that in a true democracy that claims that all men are created equal with liberty and justice for all, these kinds of things are not what should happen for generations to specific groups of people. Tipping the scales of justice to EQUALITY is what a true democratic republic strives for, amongst many other things. This cannot be the objective of a republic when the legal system is built around alternative ways to enslave and incarcerate specific people for profit.

(Side note, did you know that the term “paddy wagon” actually comes from the slave patrollers era? It did not originate in an insult or reference to Irish roots, as many people perceive. The earliest use of this phrase in Irish terms is found after 1798. Actual slaves in the early 1700s called the slave patrols “paddy rollers” because of the paddles they used to beat the slaves. It evolved to paddy wagons because of how they were transported back to plantations after the beatings.)

In this day and age, many are very quick to point out what they see as hypocrisy in citizens who push back against law enforcement's treatment of black and brown people. In other words, do not question what officers do regardless. Comments such as "how can you say black lives matter when black people kill each other?" "What about all of the abortions that black and brown women get? Do those lives matter?" "How is someone a racist because they call immigrants from Mexico rapist and murderers when the cartels in Mexico rape and murder people daily?" "You can't complain about what happens to you when you do the same to your own kind!!" This is another form of "whataboutism" we often see from people in order to avoid acknowledging issues. If you cannot see the deflection these types of questions create, along with the attempt to ignore the fact that these are the same types of crimes that ALL people commit, as well as the guilty consciousness screaming through these statements, let me help guide you.

In terms of legality, the whole argument is not to be based on what behavior average everyday citizens engage in; it is based on what officers of the law take a sworn oath to do. An officer's responsibility is to keep the peace and apprehend those who allegedly break these laws for the safety and protection of the community. Officers are not Judges, juries or executioners according to the law. Anyone who chooses to be in law enforcement has decided to shoulder this responsibility and no longer carries the same responsibilities as everyday citizens. Stop comparing what regular citizens do illegally to what those who have sworn to uphold the law and due process do. When I say what regular citizens do, I mean that whites commit the same crimes as blacks do, yet do not have the disproportionate fear or reality of being killed for not complying, not having a weapon or rightfully speaking their thoughts to officers. Why are things this way?

When a student in high school breaks the rules, they don't give themselves a 3-day suspension; the dean or the principal does that. In turn, the Dean of the school has the trust and belief of the community that they will make these decisions based on policy guidelines and fairness. What happens when you can't trust the dean or the principal to follow the rules themselves? What happens when the Dean breaks the same rules as the student? Do you then blame the students and say, "Well, students don't do what they are supposed to either, so don't come to me talking about how important students are!" "The Dean's rights matter too!" We would never ever say that.

How about if when people stand up to say that the system needs to be changed because the principal and the deans cannot be allowed to break rules and get away with it? How about if parents attacked the other parents who called for change and said that those people who hate the school system should either shut up or go away?

Can you imagine not being able to speak up on how the education system needs to improve for the benefit of those who use it? This is what happens with the legal system in this country whenever the voice comes from a minority.

Just to clarify.... Is a Police officer's job highly dangerous? Yes!! Do black people commit crimes of all kinds? Yes! Is it difficult not to lose empathy, sensitivity, and not form stereotypes in the name of your safety as an officer? ABSOLUTELY!!! Do officers deserve the utmost respect for the commitment they have sworn to uphold? HELL YEA!!

An individual makes a conscious choice to be an officer. They must be trained that crime is committed by **all** race's creeds, and colors. Losing empathy and becoming desensitized will happen without counseling or support for officers, which means that without that help, respect for the oath one takes as an officer will likely not be there. When someone betrays that oath, one must be held accountable to the same laws that others are.

No code of silence or thin blue line can erase these truths; these things only blur the line of justice.

I can tell you this.... if you ask the student who watches his teachers break all the rules that he/she is supposed to follow to then obey those same rules... we all know what we will get.

America knows what it is getting now from the youth due to its hypocrisy. We also have people who have had enough of being brutalized, labeled, all while being put front and center in a hypocrisy that simply will not stop. This is not about Marxist behavior… suburbia under attack by the big bad black criminals, or protesters using politics to further an agenda. There are people out there claiming to be justified who take advantage of any platform politically to perpetuate false narratives about minorities.

Our country's history of doing the same thing to people of color or low economic standing is clear and is repeating itself over and over again with bigger implications than before. People are tired of being abused, tired of asking not to be murdered, tired of singing and being diplomatic, only to be stomped on again. If America doesn't listen and change, America will not make it.

Law and order can only go so far when they won't acknowledge their faults and correct them.

I find it very interesting that one of the greatest symbols of law we recognize comes in the form of the "scales of Justice." I do believe that is an appropriate symbol; however, probably not for the same reasons many believe.

In my experience, the law has two ways that it can be utilized. It can be used for the people by the people or against the people by those in power. In essence, what I am saying is that law is a tool that can be used to oppress or liberate. Depending on who has their hand on the scale, that balance goes up or down to be used as a tool of favor. It shouldn't be this way, but it is.

This has been done all throughout history's societies from Rome and the senate, Congressional bodies, Parliament, to Stalin, Napoleon, Hitler, Genghis Khan, Pharaohs, Monarchs, Prime Ministers and yes, Presidents. Some have tipped the scales of law towards fair and just causes to serve the people righteously, while others sat on the scales and deemed that they themselves are the law that all must serve under. Those individuals who tipped the scales for personal benefit never seem to have a problem with law and order at that time. Those who are trampled by the law are always made out to be criminals; they are the troublemakers or the ones who need to go away if they don't like the rules. I can remember in high school when we studied about gladiators and history, they were made out to be warriors who willingly gave themselves to battle for honor. I had no idea until later in college how many of those men were rebels or slaves who spoke out against the government, who were forced by the senate (government at that time) to keep control of the masses via deflection with public combat to reduce private rebellion.

They were silenced through hand-to-hand combat and murdered to ensure the senate maintained power and control. How well did all that turn out for Rome?

You don't recognize this recurring theme?

Take a look at our country's civil war through the lens that was just painted for you, compared to Rome.... Look at how the laws worked for those people in support of the economic and physical torture of certain groups of black and brown people for centuries. Do you see it now?

Look at how the scales of justice were tipped in the name of slavery and economics. Look at what people of color were told was fair and legal? Look at what was against the law, punishable by death, often times without a judge or jury.

Look at how the law was used as a tool for those in power to further their own agenda and amass more control. What happened to those who opposed these laws and stood up? Finally, look at the cost this country paid to merely tip the scales back slightly towards a small representation of truth and justice.

The scary part is that even with all of the turmoil/death in the past we should have learned from, we are still far, far away from standing on grounds where true Law/Order and Justice exist and are practiced. It seems ironic that equal justice change continues to arrive in the form of baby steps in our country, while other government systems can and have changed overnight, depending on who is impacted by them. Again, an example of this would be how quickly laws changed around the "opioid crisis" vs the laws around the "crack era." The narrative of the names alone screams volumes in comparison, much less the arrests and incarceration laws applicable to each scenario.

PERCEPTIONS, POLITICS, PROBLEMS, PRESIDENTS & ECONOMICS THE 4Ps AND AN E.

These four Ps carry more weight than I myself realized before digging deeper into their impact. These words are all tied together by one thing at their base, and that one thing is ***PEOPLE***. Our democracy is driven by a psychology of the people that is so much more of a foundation than any of us wants to believe. It's the psychology of the *person* and the *public* that is understood and perpetuated by the educated, powerful people at the top of financial leadership.

My grandmother would always say to me, "People are smart, the public is not." For the longest time, I did not agree or, quite frankly, really understand this. I thought that "people" were not smart, and the public as a collective was smarter.

My grandmother witnessed this perspective her entire life. She saw groups of people do things that they would never subscribe to doing by themselves. As life began to show its lessons through experiences of myself and others, I learned quickly that there were many things I was wrong about when it came to "people." I found that how a person conducts themselves singularly is typically different from how they do collectively. A person who is embarrassed privately with one or two people almost always tends to have a different reaction than when being embarrassed in a large group. The realization of an achievement milestone when you are alone rarely looks the same as realizing this in the company of a group of people. When a swimmer or a track and field athlete training achieves or beats their personal best in an event, it usually garners a level of excitement, happiness, self-reflection and humble appreciation. However, when that same personal best or achievement transpires in a team setting, the reaction often is one of overwhelming, visible the top emotions and happiness. It is as if each person's actions provide fuel to another's reactions, and on and on. Even in anger, individuals are more likely to let things go if an audience is not present. The person who is disrespected or mistreated without an audience witnessing the situation is more likely to respond more levelheaded than the person on full display in front of a group. Think of how many people have found themselves in escalated altercations simply because of the image of being disrespected in front of family, friends or peers? How many have physically harmed another person simply to save face from being embarrassed in front of their peers? My thoughts over time began to change to fully agree with my grandmother. If people were more likely to make better choices when they aren't in a group setting, that spoke volumes to me about who we were as human beings. However, why do group settings corrupt so many people from what they know is right or what they would do if they were alone?

PERCEPTION is the reason that comes to mind for me.

THE TALK

Internal and external perception has been a key drivers of mankind's actions for generations. My guess would be that this has been the case since our creation. What will my wife, my family, my friends, my enemies, my employer, slaves, co-workers, teachers, fans, coaches or those on social media …. THINK OF ME? This seems to apply to every facet of our lives, as the average person is very cognizant of how they are perceived by others.

What makes this so complicated is that there is no universal path of perception. Each individual person has their own perception that follows the path they have traveled. These paths are not anchored in what is right or wrong, but more so in personal belief and personal experience. Ultimately, every person's perception becomes their own reality, often based on real-life experiences, even if the perception is completely wrong. Perception is defined as *"A way of regarding, understanding or interpreting something; a mental impression."* In essence, that means that in a country of 323 million people, give or take, there potentially are 323 million different perceptions on most of the same topics we all see and have an opinion towards. Perception is already present before individuals get involved in groups, respond to peer pressure, acceptance, anger, fear, desires, etc. The impact of where you are born, how you are raised, religious beliefs, cultural values, economic status, sexual orientation, skin color and more all play huge roles in perceptions as an individual. Since so many things are all about perception, what dictates who is right or wrong in their perception?

For me, perception has become a manipulative "label" that the power structure uses to further agendas. As a young man, I would walk down the street and watch people in their cars lock their doors as they perceived me as a dangerous threat to their safety. They did not see me as a college student, the same as they would view their own children away at school. The shock on the faces of those I would speak with when they would say, "You are so articulate". A reality I have often been told very simply, because prior to speaking with me, these individuals had never spoken to a black male before. "If you have never spoken to a black male before, why would you have this negative perception?" Being perceived as a danger to society or an uneducated idiot are but a few of the "trivial" perceptions I have encountered in this life. In all fairness, I have returned the favor by reserving negative perceptions of those I thought would have issues with me for existing in my skin. Some of my best conversations have been with men who look like poster children for the "Hells Angels" motorcycle club, and it turned out that some of those men's mindsets were nothing like what I thought. I have approached black men whom I thought I would bond with and share like concerns, only to find that they looked at me as more of a threat to them than the folks who locked the car doors on me as I walked by. Talk about perceptions shattered.... To act as though black people do not have fearful or negative perceptions of other black people is also ridiculous. Just as others do not want to be robbed or killed, we also feel the same and worry about it. Sometimes fear does mean we characterize our own kind because of the type of clothing, music, car, hairstyle or personality displayed. Often, there has been a message relayed to the public that because one lives in a lower economic environment, we choose to be ok with the crime that exists there.... complete BS by the way. The point being, no one is above the challenges that negative perceptions bring. It applies to all races, all cultures, and all people. It sucks, but it's very real, and there are no "innocent" people in terms of who has perceptions and who doesn't.

THE TALK

We have learned through history just how easy it is to alter perceptions of individuals. Especially perceptions towards lower economic citizens and people of color. For generations, the media was set in motion to only show certain people certain ways by design. This meant that you never had to actually meet an ethnic person to already know their "type" or the quality of person they were. Black people were always portrayed as slaves, maids, illiterates, degenerates, criminals or janitors, and if they had any money or wealth, they must be gangsters or drug dealers to have acquired it. This is not to say that black people cannot and have not been these not-so-great things; we have just as white people and others in other cultures have also been the exact same thing. The problem is that we were not publicly portrayed as doctors, scientists, entrepreneurs, mathematical wizards, professors in education, good fathers, stewards of the neighborhood, etc. We were also all of these things, like everyone else as well.

So, when someone saw or met a black person, they expected what they had been programmed to see. The same goes for other races. What image do you think of when I say American Indian, how about Japanese female, what about a Muslim male or a Spanish-speaking worker? I would gather that each of those persons I identified gave you an immediate picture of what you perceive them to be. While I cannot say whether your perception as an individual was a positive one or a negative one, I can say that you had an image come to you of one or the other.

Imagine being the recipient of a kind of negative perception programming that, in large part, caused judgement from those whom you had never even met? Believe it or not, this country is still fighting those old ideologies of past history, along with some new ones thrown into the mix. Negative ideologies such as slavery justification, Jim Crow voting legislation, women's suffrage movement, Japanese and Muslim internment camps for U.S born citizens, Restricted higher learning access, Civil rights battles, immigration laws applied to the majority south of the border countries, Me TOO movements, Equal pay discrimination, redlining practices, homophobia, stop and frisk legislation, racial profiling, segregation, integration, hangings, police brutality on and off video, incarceration rates, mass shootings and killings as far back as 1918 to as recent as Las Vegas over a year ago continue to take root and hold. Depending on how a lot of these subjects are manipulated by those in power, I suppose there can be a lot of fear generated towards certain people.

Did you know that prior to 1860, there were a lot of white citizens who privately believed slavery was wrong? However, once they were in large crowds of the public, they "went along to get along" until things got to the point where that just wasn't going to work anymore.

The number of gatherings for hangings and public executions during the 1800s to this day cannot be accurately accounted for; however, the eyewitness accounts told by so many who claimed to find these displays of death and mutilation despicable shed some light on the volume of occurrences. Many of these people knew that if they didn't participate, they would be perceived as sympathizers or traitors and could find themselves hanging from the same rope. Now that's a hell of a situation to find yourself in, don't you think? Be wholesome at home, but be a barbarian in public in front of your family, thus teaching them to be the same. Celebrate the man hanging from the rope or share the noose next to him. Damn.... that's a hell of a thing, isn't it? Talk about the power of fear and perception.

Beyond all of this, think of the power an entity could have if it could use this concept on groups to its benefit to support their agenda. The ability to make people accept concepts that, individually, they may disagree with, but in public, perceive that they have to support. Welcome to the world of **POLITICS.**

Over the years, I have come to learn and understand that there is truly an art to being an effective politician. Everyone cannot do it successfully. Some of the most corrupt, soulless people have gotten away with implementing heinous policies and choices behind mastering politics. "The manipulation of people and processes." Convincing people to go along with your agenda based on perception and group mentality has become the hallmark of Republican vs Democrat debates. Truth doesn't matter anymore, only perception. A politician is fully aware that they are lying about a topic, but as long as it appeals to the viewers' perception, desire and acceptance, the truth simply doesn't matter. An individual wants to be part of something,

especially if they believe they have a place on that winning team of that something. People will forsake right and wrong, decency, character and humanity to simply be on that team and win. Just look at how many have been on the wrong side of history due to this.

If I am going to talk about this and be transparent, I must come out and say that the overwhelming majority of politicians of **all parties** manipulate, give disinformation and use these tactics to get a leg up on opponents. This is done to get the financial support they will need for the policies they look to implement. Policies that are often lucrative due to lobbyist groups that ensure financial backing in return for said policies. From Obama to Bush, Trump to Clinton, Kennedy to Reagan, the game is played the same by folks in all of these administrations, just on different sides of the political aisle. While I, too, have had political figures that I favored and respected, there is always that reserve I keep for understanding that being a politician has certain meanings and implications that cannot be ignored. Just as there are two sides to every coin, it is so with this profession, and one of the sides is simply not a positive one. It seems that repeatedly, so many of us citizens do not give the proper credit to politicians for the power of manipulation they actually have. I do not know if it's because we don't realize it or because we don't want to see how things continue to go the way of the politician in a system supposedly designed to reflect the agenda of the people. Or is it that we just don't pay enough attention to what is done and executed legislatively versus what is promised to us? I find it amazing that the American people can be upset about an issue that politicians will agree with us on publicly and verbally, but then vote for a policy or a law that goes completely against that understanding. "What in the hell are you talking about, that doesn't happen?" is what you may be saying right now.

How about two examples of this? As of today, one of the biggest challenges we have in this country is homelessness. We have about 600,000 homeless people in the United States. About 25% of those people suffer from Severe mental illness, another 3rd suffer from mental illness that is not severe but requires medical treatment. That's about 350,000 people who are homeless with some kind of mental illness. In 1994, most state-run mental institutions ran out of federal funding and closed their doors all across the country. Every politician will stand up in front of us and spew about how they care about the plight of the homeless and mentally ill. They talk about how to help them and make things better so that we can be proud of how our country takes care of our less fortunate, and then they go and vote on a policy to close the very institutions that keep the mentally ill and the general public safe. The kicker is.... we the people say nothing about their decision and then complain about all the “crazy homeless” people in the street. Makes one wonder who is really crazy, doesn’t it? I grew up near a mental hospital called Central State, which was known not only for the housing of severely mentally ill patients but also for the widespread treatment of those with mental challenges who could function in society as long as they had access to regular treatments. Guess what happened to them, ALL of them, when the hospital closed? No outpatient treatments, no medicine dispersed and no hospitalization for those who needed that protected environment. All were released, most with nowhere or no one to go. Is that what great leaders do to their citizens all across the board? Is that what the citizens settle for and accept? As long as it was about budgets and money, the answer was and still is yes.

The second example is the same scenario, only substitute the homeless who are mentally ill with our veterans, who are also often ignored, mistreated, misrepresented and left homeless as well. While in this day and age, there are younger politicians fighting for better treatment of veterans than before, the long-standing mantra of “if it costs too much money, the answer is no” still remains the headline. Imagine if the same politicians who vote to send you to war or the Middle East or to whatever conflict being used to take other countries' resources are also the same politicians who vote to decrease funding for medical care to treat the aftereffects of fighting wars where they sent you? Again, we accept this behavior from politicians as citizens and voters. That is…. until many of us decide to be halfcocked, fair-weather, fake patriots screaming about the flag and the sacrifices of the soldiers we drive right past under the bridge every day. ALMOST ALL OF US DRIVE BY THEM AND PRAY THE LIGHT DOESN'T

TURN RED. Because when we are alone, we know we are wrong, but with are political group, we scream about patriotism that we don't live up to. All because we want to support the agenda of someone else for the sake of perception or being on the winning team in power. Refusing to stand for what's right and acknowledge what's wrong.

Tough to hear, isn't it? Of course, everything doesn't apply to everyone, and there are plenty of people who stand up for veterans, the mentally ill and injustice, but clearly not the overwhelming majority, because if that were the case, things would simply be different. Things are not different.

How do we continue to allow those in positions we voted to put them in to continue to misrepresent doing what is right? Why are we ok with allowing behaviors like this or worse to continue? How can we claim to be a civilized society yet watch a man being murdered publicly on our televisions in our faces, not by a citizen breaking the law, but by a law enforcement officer? How can so many citizens ignore that what they saw take place in front of the world has been an ongoing occurrence to specific groups of people on camera and off camera for GENERATIONS? How can we expect the groups that have endured this to continue to accept the inequality and treatment of our Wives, Mothers, daughters, Sisters, and Nieces in the workplace, financially and physically? Fathers bury their sons, brothers, uncles, nephews, grandfathers and neighbors daily with no apology, empathy or accountability in justice. Why is a person labeled a "bleeding-heart liberal" if you stand up for humanity? If you stand up for the environment when it's clear that everyone knows the planet is in trouble because of our pollution? Doesn't everyone breathe? Don't we all need water to survive? Shouldn't "bleeding heart" be in front of any political affiliation when it comes to human beings? When did it become a bad thing to care about the well-being of people, the environment we live in, to stand against death and brutality from all threats, especially those who are sworn to protect and serve us? Why is it a bad thing to stand up for the fair treatment of one of humanity's most precious parts of creatures in it... the woman? Without her, we no longer exist. It seems as though the need to win at all costs and amass money for those in power takes a front seat over everything.

If we are truly honest with ourselves, we cannot really blame the politicians as much as we would like to, because they only do what we let them. We task them with solving our problems the way they see fit instead of holding them accountable to represent the views of the people who got them elected. They simply take our problems and solve them the way they perceive it should be done, which often only benefits a small percentage of the population. We call that the 1 percent. The PEOPLE need to enact their right to find fair representation to enact true and just solutions to our ***PROBLEMS.***

Of course, one cannot solve any problem until one can acknowledge that there actually is the existence of one. What does that mean? There are a lot of problems that are swept under the rug. This particular problem is about surviving being a child of color. Well.... If only 16% of the population are aware of or have “The talk” with their kids about how to come home alive after dealing with systemic oppression and law enforcement, that probably means that a good 75% of the population don’t know or believe there is a problem that requires “The talk.” If I don’t see it as a problem in my world, how is it really a problem? That is the perception of reality for 75% of the population, who simply do not have to deal with that reality. The crazy part about this is that both of those perceptions are real. Simultaneously, both of those actual realities also exist. One is not a problem for the 75% while the other problem for that 16% is very real. Failure to acknowledge problems when they don't apply to you continues to give way to the destruction of our society as a whole.

COVID-19, Unemployment rates, Furlough rates, police brutality, voter suppression, Gender discrimination, White supremacy, violent protesters, domestic violence, drug abuse, systemic racism, criminal justice and sentencing laws, healthcare for the sick.... These are just a few of the real problems that this country continues to face every day. Because some of these problems don't impact certain people, certain people choose to act as though the problems don't exist or are not of true consequence.

It is not until one of these problems suddenly occurs in a citizen's circle that they acknowledge the problem and its impact. There are examples of this everywhere, just ask Chris Christie or Herman Cain (if you could) about COVID-19 sickness. Not to be funny or disrespectful, however, the truth is that Mr Cain disregarded the seriousness of this virus for what seems to be perception, and it cost him his life. How about asking 15-year veteran Federal Officer Ms. Jackson about her police profiling interaction with another officer during a traffic stop on July 21st in Alabama? Is that officer-on-officer crime? How about the courthouse that was burned down by instigators during a protest about George Floyd? Though many media outlets stated protesters were responsible, they were not. Did anyone acknowledge the propaganda problem around this situation? How about the fact that domestic violence rose 22% in the first 4 months of the pandemic, and instead of being proactive with awareness and solutions, what did we do? We waited for politicians to make it a partisan issue and point the finger around who votes to get us back to "normal" faster in the middle of a damn global pandemic! Are we really this stupid? (Me included) These are but a few of the problems that we were facing, as the list goes on and on. Ultimately, no matter what is going on in the world, the big three in this country are always the selective problems that some must embrace, and others ignore. DRUG ABUSE, RACISM, CRIME. Again, typically it is not until one of these problems ends up in one's personal circle that it really demands one to pay attention or care about the subject. But rest assured, these three problems can always be tracked back to being what contributes to more heartbreak and death than most any other problems on the board.

One of the most interesting things is how those with money and power manipulate and transfer the existence of these problems to specific groups of people based on economic status or race. (Economic stature and race are one in the same in the eyes of power; some races have been fooled into believing it is not.) Thus, begging the question from those in power, "What problems?" This is what certain layers of power in American society say about the things they know exist, like its plausible deniability. In all fairness, there are a lot of secular citizens not in power who really do not know about these problems other than what they see on the screens of their phones, computers or televisions.

I have many acquaintances and colleagues who, when faced with these problems for the first time, make a deer looking at headlights seem highly self-aware. Again, in my opinion, that is what happened with a huge population of the country when George Floyd was murdered on TV in front of us all. So many people were beyond shocked and appalled, unable to believe that this could happen. Problems that simply don't apply to certain groups of people seemed unfathomable. To those of us who have seen this our entire existence and heard about it from previous family members as early as we can remember in our existence, this was not anywhere near a new occurrence. How can the problems impacting some be resolved when the masses don't see a problem?

When it comes to tools that politics uses to solve problems, there is no other tool that has been more misused, impactful and destructive to those without power than ***PRISONS***. Be it a mental restraint, such as parole or the highly publicized physical incarceration of one kind or another, our country has been at the forefront of using prisons as problem solutions for almost everything. Everything except serving fair, equal justice and or rehabilitating an individual while paying for their crimes against our society or humanity. After all, didn't we say that was the purpose of incarceration? To put it bluntly, prisons have simply been widely used as a tool of oppression and power. This has been executed under the cloak of an immoral justice system designed to widely target certain groups of people based on economic position and the complexion of their skin. Wow... now that's a mouthful! I know there are many who would disagree with that sentence, and rightfully so!

If your life and those around you have never been impacted this way, you will definitely yell "FOUL" to this statement, as you should. However, just because it's not in your circle doesn't mean it doesn't exist or disappear. In the early 1800s and late 1700s, most people in the northern part of the United States had no idea of the true horrors taking place against human beings in the South. Those who were aware of this prison of slavery ignored it as it wasn't their concern and didn't impact their life. By 1860, it was a different story, though and suddenly it became something that would impact the lives of the entire nation economically and physically. Then everyone started to care one way or another.

For so many people of color, the true birth of incarceration and prison began with slavery, then in the early 1700s with "slave patrollers", which later became groups of "lawmen sent to apprehend" so-called fugitives. The loss of money and power after the Civil War and the Emancipation Proclamation was devastating to those who held black people as property. So, wouldn't you know that shortly thereafter, a law was passed that stated that one was free unless they committed a felony crime. If they were convicted of said felony crime, they could be placed back in the same conditions the Emancipation Proclamation supposedly freed them from. Guess what suddenly, magically exploded in this country? Crimes committed by people of color. The apprehension, arrest and conviction rates of certain people were suddenly through the roof as "slavery was abolished except for the convicted felon." Not to say that there were never true crimes committed or true criminals apprehended in the equation; however, the data is very available as to the majority of those incarcerated and why.

Most were handed ridiculously long sentences for fictitious petty charges, making it clear that the free labor chain gangs and prison plantation camps garnered for accountability were simply a different label from the "slave plantation." Prisons became a for-profit generating entity as soon as plantation labor with slaves was illegal, and they still are to this day. This was the replacement of the "livestock" that the South lost in the war.

Whether we like it or not, you can trace all of the unjust practices of law enforcement and prisons to the models that were used starting back in the 1700s, to the adjustments after the Civil War and the Emancipation Proclamation. The practice of arresting and convicting black people to put them back into servitude was established by the high rates of who was targeted and how much time they were given for crimes most often not committed. The concepts of stop and frisk, racial profiling, planting evidence, assault and abuse in police stops, murder by law enforcement, unexplained deaths of inmates, due process not granted, sentencing expanded under false pretenses and on were born through this. This is 100% relative to the arrest rates and incarceration numbers amongst people of color that you still see to this very day. The volume of law abiding citizens who were placed in jail for offenses such as looking a white person in the eye, reading in public, speaking an opinion out loud, looking at any female that is white if you are not white, possession of anything too nice became an accusation of theft, talking back or being perceived as sarcastic in communication were offenses that would get you arrested and convicted for YEARS. Where do you think the culture of "don't talk back to police or correctional officers" came from? How about "lock you up and throw away the key?" Literally, you could be hung by police officers and or spectators on the spot just because someone didn't like how you crossed the street. To put it in perspective, my mother could have been arrested had she walked in the front door of certain stores or restaurants. Did you read what I said...my mother. Not my grandmother or great grandmother or great, great grandmother. We aren't talking about Jim Crow ALONG TIME AGO……. ARRESTED FOR WALKING IN THE FRONT DOOR OF AN ESTABLISHMENT BECAUSE COLOREDS ONLY CAN GO TO THE BACK. You could have gone to prison for that. My mother could have been in jail for years behind that kind of offense, but more importantly, a whole lot of mothers and fathers did go to jail for that very same thing. This is actually how criminal justice was originally designed to function, ending in the incarceration of those that the system was originally created to keep enslaved.

Why am I belaboring this point, you may ask? Well, this is how these kinds of trumped-up offenses have been handled towards people of color for generations, so how do you think real crimes such as murder and rape have been handled regarding white citizens who committed them? How fair do you think those trials have been to their victims? How balanced were the years of those prison sentences given out compared to what a Black person received for drinking out of the wrong water fountain? The sentencing for two thieves, one person of color and one not. Do you think they were ever equal in sentencing for the conviction of the same crimes? I know you already know the answer because it happens to this very day.

So, if we go back to the big three problems of DRUG ABUSE, RACISM AND CRIME, how do you think prisons come into play in dealing with these challenges? Prisons are the tools to ensure the playing field is never level, while capitalising at the same time.

Does this mean that I believe there should be no prisons? No incarcerations for crimes committed. No accountability for doing harm to others or breaking laws? ABSOLUTELY NOT!! The question for all is simply this: how do you stand behind a system that is so implicitly biased? How can I? A system that has been this way for so long that it seems it cannot change to be fair and just for those who truly should be held accountable. How can a system like this be trusted or supported to deliver justice and accountability?

There are so many options to analyze how our prisons and justice systems have never been fair and just, but I will focus on these topics. The Crack epidemic of the 80s vs the Opioid crisis of the 2000s/ Dylan Roof's mass shooting vs Columbine Mass shooting vs DC sniper/Bill Cosby sexual harassment vs Harvey Weinstein sexual harassment/ Charlottesville murder vs 17-year-old Portland shooting. Lastly, the difference between how unarmed protesters who “step” out of line or not are handled vs militias that arrive at state capitols armed, demanding that policies change. The rules are simply not the same.

Drug use, abuse and solicitation is undoubtedly one of this country's biggest problems. It is an age-old problem that has done nothing but thrive due to the lack of true solutions. Unfortunately, true solutions would have too much of a negative monetary impact on those who actually profit the most from it. Even though its impact affects all citizens, that doesn’t seem to change the implementation of viable solutions. From 1980 to 1986, drug charges and convictions increased by 134%. Can you guess who received the heftiest sentences of that 134%? Heroin and cocaine cases increased from 2,677 in 1980 to 7,769 in 1986, which put them at the root cause of most drug crimes. Believe it or not, this is not the biggest problem during the 80s. The bigger problem becomes the number of murders and addictions that transpired in the wake of the drug activity. Crack cocaine annihilated entire neighborhoods and communities, tearing families apart with no help or support in sight. Dead or in jail were the two options that most people faced who engaged in the use of the substance. Male, female, adult or child made no difference and garnered no empathy from society on the outcomes of those involved in this way of life. Whether you were in its direct path of its effect or a bystander, it was all your fault. Did you know that overdoses from cocaine rarely happened before crack hit the scene? Also, did you know that prior to crack hitting the urban environment, gun manufacturers' production of weapons under the cost of $100 was down? At the same time, homicides of young black men were also down prior to crack's emergence. 1986 sparked the increase of all three, which continued to spike for ten years after that. Production of guns under $100 went from 150,000 in 1985 to 300,000 in 1986, plateauing at 900,000 produced in late 1993. Homicides among young black men followed the same pattern, spiking in 1986 with continued growth to a high in 1994 with a death rate of 200 per 100,000, creating a 120% increase from 1980.

Lastly, cocaine overdoses were at ZERO from 1980 to roughly late 1985, early 1986, when the increase began at a rate of about 10 per 100,000. The rate gained more traction, climbing to a rate above 150 per 100,000 by 1993. By 1998, the rate had grown to 200 per 100,000 in not just black people, but all races, before it began to descend in the year 2000. During this time frame, the only prominent program was "The War on Drugs." It was not about medical support, rehabilitation programs, addiction aptitude or family counseling to mend the destruction in economically depressed communities.

Homelessness, mental illness, crack babies, crack mothers, HIV/AIDS infections all ran rampant through these communities with little to no support, empathy or assistance from the government other than arrests and jail sentences. In short, from 1986 to about 1999 the verdict on most people caught up in or participating in the crack epidemic was "too bad, so sad" and you either ended up dead, in jail, an addict or homeless. Collateral damage of communities in the response to the "crack epidemic" said to be unavoidable by those that some say ushered in this era. How telling is it that the very administration that unofficially perpetuated this phenomenon are the same ones that declared the "war on drugs." One may be surprised to check into how many billions of dollars were made from 1985 to 1996 in the drug trade, who actually profited the most and where that money went.

As cocaine overdoses began to decline in 2000, ***Opioid overdoses via prescription*** started their ascent in 1999. To think that the crack era and the Opioid era were not intertwined is a mistake, as they surely were. About ten years later (2010), heroin overdoses also started to rise again, but at a much slower rate than it did in the previous years. Evolution peaks and prevails around 2013 with synthetic Opioid overdoses hitting the scene.

Rising to a new high, we see prescription opioids and heroin all in 2017, marking the true impact of the Opioid crisis. Heroin and synthetic Opioids stayed under the radar for years, which meant no "war on drugs" for those products; meanwhile, prescription drugs were out in the open, with episodes here and there of publicized overdoses.

These situations always seemed to be smoothed over in the public eye or swept under the rug, depending on who overdosed, until the occurrences could no longer be ignored. One of the reasons why things could no longer be ignored is very simply because of who was dying. As before in the beginning stages of crack, a lot of money was being made in multiple markets, legal and illegal. However, the participant profile drastically changed from the lower economic environment to the middle- and upper-class economic structure. As the youth say these days, ***"it hits a bit different"*** when it's a different economic class of people impacted, especially the younger generation. Dope fiends just don't look the same to everyone when they are from suburbia.

Ultimately, the vantage point those in power had on these PROBLEMS that were taking place when it was crack, allowed them to review solutions and options they implemented for themselves and those that looked like them. The implementation of those in power historically to battle drug abuse changed with the demographics of the opioid user. That change was a supported, elevated gesture towards humanity with the change of the President and his politics. It suddenly mattered in a different way. The tone of how things will proceed in a nation is often set by the **PRESIDENT** in power at the time. While most do not understand that presidents really do not wield as much power as the House of Representatives and the Senate, most people do understand and respond to the *INFLUENCE* that a president can have. This position of power is one that can be used to educate and motivate, or to deceive and misinform. A president can use laws as an ally to the people or as a weapon to instil fear, anger and retaliation amongst the people. A nation often looks to a president as a guide, offering a sense of direction, purpose and the belief that regardless of what is happening, things will ultimately be ok with the right plan and approach.

More so than a power position, it is a trusted position that holds the sentiments of the people who believed enough to vote and elect a person they felt would look out for the best interest of them and all who are present in the country they live in. Not to be perfect, not to never make mistakes, but to want to do what is best for all.

Shouldn't a president be someone that we want our children to emulate? Someone who we would love to work for in a day-to-day, normal job capacity? Someone who, at least on the surface, we would trust has gone through some of our experiences and understands what it means to exist in this country? I would think that is something that every person in a nation could get behind.

True enough, some of the challenges transpire when each person's experiences come into play. We have Atheists, pro-choice, pro-life, religious faiths, Racists, homophobic, bigots, chauvinists, elitists, educated, uneducated, unskilled workers, skilled workers, dialects of English, Spanish, French, Arabic, Chinese, Japanese, southern mindsets, northern mindsets, east coast vs west coast and on and on...... Truth is, some experiences of the people are illegal, immoral and unethical, while others are just different based on how they were raised or where. Finding a president who will be mindful of the entire nation and not specifically the ones who put in the votes for victory is no easy task.

To act as though we all don't have agendas is beyond naïve; we do. To act as though an agenda is not destroying us is irresponsible, not sustainable and quite frankly, insanity. When people in a country cannot have a conversation and disagree without name-calling or resorting to physical violence, that's the leadership's fault. When a nation is so divided that we see each other as enemies domestically, and that is encouraged, that's leadership's fault. When we make excuses for the death and destruction of our own people and when we know that injustice is running amok in our streets, that's leadership's fault. When the narrative is that we overlook the resolution in order to blame the victims and the reactions of those impacted, that's the fault of leadership. Most importantly, when we forsake the things that we have lived through, knowing what truth is just too then support false ideologies, this is not only the fault of leadership, it's the failure of the people.

How does a nation get to the point that it ignores the truths posed directly to its face? How does a nation forget a pandemic that's supposed to disappear in weeks and does not? How do educated people follow behind anyone who tells them ten months later they should be thankful for the vaccine they made happen? A vaccine for the same pandemic they stated was a hoax, and that would disappear. How do you give credit to someone who uses said vaccine but doesn't impart how important it is that all of his constituents do the same? Applauds them when they go against the very system trying to keep them alive, even though he claims to have created that same system.

How do we as a nation allow anyone to defend those who are on the side of racially charged rhetoric and death? Am I not mistaken, or was there not a full-on civil war behind this concept? Yes, it's correct that one of the ways one should combat racism is without violence and physical confrontation; however, when racism and supremacy become increasingly violent, what should happen then? Is that when we talk about how there are good people on both sides? Are we also to say that there were good slave owners? Masters that were fair because they only beat their slaves when they made mistakes, not just because they felt like it? Hasn't it already been established that if you are on the side of racism and supremacy, you are simply wrong? Law enforcement is supposed to try to rectify challenges with civility, respect and without incident when possible? When they cannot do so because citizens unwarranted choose to shoot at them, stab them or attack them, there is never any confusion about how they have to respond to such violence. Never has a president stated that there were good people on both sides when it was clear who was breaking the law. Shouldn't we have a president who understands the rule of law but also knows that lawmakers are not above the same laws? Law enforcement officers are accountable when they break the law. And yes, when citizens are brutalized by anyone, included law enforcement, they will fight back and defend themselves as they have a legal right to do so. A president who acknowledges that citizens doing things such as shooting random police officers in Dallas is against the law and is not the answer or the right thing to do. Law enforcement officers also have families and should not be shot down randomly in response to anger. However, a President must also speak to how police officers cannot continue killing unarmed people of color over and over again. Addressing all of this is not the same as saying there are good people on both sides; it requires demanding accountability of all involved in a conflict. These are unarmed citizens are sons, daughters, mothers, fathers, brothers, sisters, nieces and nephews of people who love them. Unjustly taking lives away from families cannot be deemed the work of "good police officers."

There are no good people on both sides of situations like this. There are simply bad people who believe they are protected in doing bad things, and then there are the people who are left to react to those bad things that have been executed. A simple example to bring clarity. If someone kills a man's son for no reason, that individual is a bad person.

True, we should not take the law into our own hands, nor should we kill anyone, according to what some religions tell us. The reality of this situation is, many fathers will probably attempt to kill the bad person and anyone who was involved in taking their child away. Do we then say that there were good people on both sides in this situation? Accountability for both sides? You would think that a leader, especially a President, would understand these complexities and be mindful of that in the banter they utilize. That requires character.

Often, I think about one of the Presidential candidates whomm I was never a big fan of, but knew that if he became president, he would at least try to do the right thing for everyone. The reason why I felt this way was because of a situation I saw him handle, which was probably against his own interests.

John McCain was at a town hall when a woman stood up and called Barack Obama a Muslim and a terrorist. Now, he could have just skipped her comment and let it ride, which would have undoubtedly fueled more people to vote for him. (We know this to be fact because this tactic has been utilized since then) Instead, Senator McCain politely corrected the woman in a way that allowed her to keep her dignity in place while firmly letting her know that her statement was not true. That Barack Obama was not Muslim, not a terrorist and in fact a good man who loves this country. Even though this man wasn't my choice for President, I could have gotten behind him if he had won, simply because he embodied the principle of trust in the position. A guide of hope and motivation in the face of racism and bigotry that can do nothing but destroy us all. Not saying he was a saint or that he supported policies I thought were great, but he did show the character of being someone I would work with in the day-to-day journey to improve this nation. That quality resonated with me. Plus, when everyone attacked him for being fair and honest, that provided confirmation that I knew he was a man of character. Our society always attacks those kinds of people.

It's my belief that he would have spoken out against those officers shown on body cams killing unarmed people of color. He would not stand alongside hate groups of any kind, rising up to attack citizens simply because they were different. I don't think he would have been silent when groups planned to abduct and murder government officials. For some reason, I just can't see Senator McCain not react ASAP to a virus that had the ability to cause death in so many other countries BEFORE it came here and not sound the alarm to all of us. Somehow, I just don't think he would have had to fire so many people from his administration and then pardon almost a dozen of them for breaking multiple federal laws.

There is no way that I could see him compromising the laws and the will of the people just to overturn a decision he didn't like. I am not making him out to be some saint, my great white hope or anything like that. For all I know, maybe I am way off base here. From watching what he displayed overall, my vibe was that he was an honorable man, for whatever that's worth.

This is the kind of quality I want in a candidate, especially if the person I choose to vote for loses. My perception of what being president is probably differs from what many Americans think of when they consider a president. It is not a glamorous job like being a Hollywood celebrity. It doesn't pay them millions of dollars as an independent business tycoon would expect to get paid. Most don't consider the responsibility of the 323 plus million lives you are ultimately responsible for in this role.

Whose dream is it to send men and women soldiers to war and conflict that most will not come back alive or the same? Trying to negotiate with countries that hate our guts, either because of the past things we did to them or simply because our politics and lifestyles give the impression that we look down on them. The red tape of political parties fighting each other internally for control of power, big companies and lobbyists that have more pull in law-making than you do, and pressures of being mindful that entities that you piss off could end up getting you assassinated, similar to John F Kennedy. Does this sound like a dream job to anyone? Being the face of a country as a President also means the nation's wins or losses in the present and the past become your wins and losses. This country has a big history full of many amazing achievements and horrific occurrences. Every president leaves a mark on this country that **history** will record as a success or failure, moral or immoral, valiant or cowardly.

What's more interesting is the fact that the economic impact a President has during their term is typically more notable in history than the social impact a President has. Economics will always carry more weight than any President. Why is that?

Very simply, the history of **ECONOMICS** is quite frankly the source of **everything** that has transpired, positive or negative, since Europeans set foot in North America. Do you know what the definition of economics is? For the longest time, I thought I knew and understood, but I did not. The best definition I found is noted as: *the branch of knowledge concerned with the production, consumption and transfer of wealth.*

Let that sink in and ask yourself if that definition is what you think of when someone speaks of economics. Do you think of businesses, government budgets, Wall Street, the national deficit, currency, or any of the things we are told are the heart of economics? The first four words in the definition are as clear as a bell when you read them. Those words represent why so many of us are so far behind the eight ball of life. We don't realize that KNOWLEDGE is the most important component in economics. This is one of the main reasons why it's been so easy for those in power to pit so many of us against each other.

Economics is at the top of the food chain over every component when it comes to our society. Racism, sexism, bigotry, crime, homelessness, sickness, unemployment, war, politics, government, religion and everything you can think of are tools of economics. Those in power recognize these tools; they also know that the public at large doesn't recognize these things in the same way. The impact of the knowledge one has or does not have is literally life-changing. More importantly, knowledge like this or lack thereof is life-binding. Meaning white and black citizens alike have been bound to poverty together, all the while not actually realizing we are in the same boat.

Some of the most exciting conversations I have ever had with people who do not look like me have been about economics. It was exciting to me because often in those conversations, I was the only one who understood that everything we were really talking about was economics.

The topic of rich celebrities and athletes is always one that gets interesting for me in discussions. What often feels like justification comments, such as "Look at how many athletes are millionaires these days! Look how far this country has come! How can you say that progress hasn't been made?" First, it is important to acknowledge and congratulate all of the talented athletes who worked their asses off and sacrificed childhood and teenage years to become enough of an expert in their craft to EARN the lifestyle that comes with being a professional athlete. No one GAVE them anything other than the **chance to compete**. That is the progress that has been made, the opportunity to compete.

Second, it is important to know that in these conversations I have had, the reference points were always directed at athletes of color. Clearly, it's not necessary for anyone to act as though societal progress pertains to white people being millionaires in any capacity. These talks became a quest for others to show me how much better life for people of color had become. Through selective memory, millions of people tend to forget that not too long ago, people of color were denied even the CHANCE to compete for spots in sports, much less ones that truly provided high revenue streams. Economics is the reason those opportunities have come about, not a moral awakening in society.

Collegiate or professional sports all operate the same way, with economics being the primary driver, with talent coming in second. Professional team owners are driven by the revenue their teams generate on many different platforms, such as TV ratings and viewership, Arena or dome sales, merchandise sales, value or retail worth of the franchise, partnerships with national and local businesses, international endorsements and more. The consumer also demands to see certain variables in a professional team to maintain their social interest and financial spend. Some of those demands that had to be met have evolved over time from just being a fan of an "all-American sport" to demanding a team to have competitive, viable high high-performing players. This demand truly ushered in the era of the black athlete at the collegiate and professional levels. Most colleges did not have any black athletes until the 1940s, while the NFL didn't see its first black player until 1949. Of course, Major League Baseball saw a significant change in Jackie Robinson in 1947, with the exception of Moses Fleet Walker, another black athlete who played a season in 1889 with the Toledo Blue Jays.

As the dynamic of the players changed, so did the competition and the ability to win. The mix of players of color with the existing white players began to create championships and dynasties that sports had never seen. Colleges and professional sports saw the demand from consumers to watch these games skyrocket as they had never before. Instantly, this demand was monetized to billions for the sporting industry, which meant significant salaries for the standout players.

Some of the same players that this country previously would have despised, feared, hated and would rather see swinging from a noose, suddenly became the most beloved Americans **while they were playing their sport**. By the 1960s, colleges in states that were populated with citizens who rejected and detested black people ended up being the same ones that were diehard fans for their state's football, basketball and baseball teams. Teams that had black athletes woven through them boosted the chances for colleges to win.

Economics that had put us against each other since the 1600s now brought us together, if only for four quarters, two halves, a halftime show or nine innings by the 1970s. To this day, the revenue that collegiate and professional teams generate comes from all races of people who remain die-hard fans for their team of choice. People who normally can't stand the sight of each other put on their favorite jerseys and unite to pay homage to and celebrate their team competing. All of this only to go back at each other's throats once the game is over. Meanwhile, guess who continues to rake in the dough, expanding their wealth? I'll give you one guess, and it's not those fans. How dumb are we?

The majority of people who are racist do not have any more wealth than the people they are prejudice against. Imagine groups of people living the same kind of life, suffering the same kind of poverty, attacking each other over skin color. The trailer park vs the projects, a crack head vs a meth head, the homeboy vs the redneck and yet we think we are so different. We suffer from a lack of education, lack of resources, quality healthcare and reside in crime-ridden areas because we can't afford to go anywhere else. A poor white farmer suffers the same fate as a poor black farmer, yet they both are controlled by the person who chooses to purchase or not purchase the products each farmer grows. They are both subject to how much those in power choose to pay for their goods, as well as the determination of what they are worth. One day, I was speaking with someone I worked with, and we had this conversation about economics and race. Now, this conversation was more relevant to the Jim Crow era than it would be to current times, as I said to him, "You know that we are the have-nots, made to look stupid by those that have." He asked me what I meant by that, so I told him a story about a grocery store in the 1950s.

In the 1950s, there was a grocery store in a small southern town, very much under Jim Crow law. Now, from early morning to around 4 pm, whites would enter the store and purchase items, drink from the water fountain, use the bathroom if needed and go on about their business. From 5 pm to 7 pm, black people were allowed to enter the store from the back entrance, purchase items they needed, use the bathroom out back or drink from the water hose out back and go on about their business as well. The white citizens weren't fond of knowing black people came inside the store in the evening, and the blacks did not like that because of the white people; they had to use the back of the store and only enter at the end of the day just to be able to buy things. The animosity between the two parties was clear. You know who didn't care about any of this and was happy about it all? The owner of the store. You see, he was able to raise the prices, dictate what to sell, who to sell it to and get money from both the black customers and the white customers. Unfortunately, they didn't pay attention to how wealthy they made the store owner because they were too busy worrying about disliking each other.

Immediately, the person I worked with understood and said, "Sonofabitch! This is how we get played against each other." I told him that the kicker to this day is that the store owner makes you feel good because you look like him, but he still controls the prices and the products for you, just as he does for me. You unite with the owner over familiarity, while suffering the same economic fate as I, the black person. The have-nots.

THE TALK

Economics and politics are probably my favorite topics simply because of how intriguing it has been to watch government officials convince white people and others who consider themselves different from people of color to vote against their own well-being. It's actually economic genius when you think about it. In talking with another colleague of mine, it was said that "it's a shame that so many black and Latino people are on welfare. It doesn't help them get on their feet, and they are just bleeding the system that you and I pay for." It was interesting that this person felt comfortable enough to say that to me in the first place, but it piqued my curiosity, so I asked if they thought government assistance was a small, medium or large problem in this country. The person thought it was a large problem, stating that if more blacks and Latinos would get off welfare, stop being homeless and lazy, it would save millions of dollars for us all. Again, I thought to myself, do people think race disappears with a decent paycheck? "Hello…I am black," as I chuckled to myself. My next question was about the origin of this belief and why they thought this was true. The response of the origin was around the politicians and pundits this person saw on Fox News regularly, who stated that citizens should vote to cut welfare and government assistance programs because so many minorities defraud the system and don't really need it. Also, they stated that every time the news shows people on welfare, it's always black people, so this person was convinced that they would definitely vote for a conservative republican to cut those wasteful benefits.

This is when things got interesting…. Would it be ok if I showed you some data on welfare and government assistance in this country? I asked? Imagine the shock when I physically showed the individual that these programs are used majority by white Americans? Of the 59 million people in this country on just some of these programs in 2022, 43% are white and 23% are black. The rest is split between Latino, Asian and Native Americans. Not to mention the additional 13 million citizens who live in poverty who don't receive any kind of benefits. Then came my next question of how many Asian or Latino homeless people have you seen in your life? Now, I know this happens and exists in parts of this country; however, I have not seen this after living in six states. Neither had the person with whom I was speaking. Clearly, that perception is based on a singular purview, but the point was made. Ultimately, this person was prepared to vote to cut benefits for a program that serves a majority of people who were not minorities, simply because of the media and politics. Having done no research, being misled by those in power who would have you believe that you are elevated above these minorities, when the truth is that minorities would be less impacted than the white Americans you identify with. Outside of the fact that it sucks that anyone would deny another person's basic essentials to exist because of color, it's even worse that one can be persuaded to do so through media influence. Do you understand the kind of economic influence those in power possess to make a person vote to hurt their own interests? To use the tools of racism and prejudice to manipulate and blind someone into believing that putting more money in a politician's pocket is worth it, as long as minorities are impacted? Then only to find out that not only does it hurt others who really need help, but it also hurts you and your distant neighbor you identify with? The American public truly doesn't understand the power we allow ourselves to be governed by. Needless to say, my colleague was blown out of the water by this. The realization that this person had many, many friends and colleagues who felt the same way, planning to vote the same way, based on manipulation and false data, shook them to the core. Economics knows that the veil of racism and hate is much too thick for most people to see the truth through. Its purpose has been and continues to be served extremely well, while we all continue to fight for crumbs to survive.

"Do you have an idea of who truly bears the lion's share of the tax burden of keeping this country afloat, but I'm scared of your answer", I stated to my colleague. At this point, I could see that uncertainty was setting in and plaguing every aspect of what they thought they knew, so

The response was a resounding question mark. Well, you already know it's not the rich because they get so many tax breaks that we are lucky if they pay 15% of their total income. It can't be the poor, as we just discussed how government assistance and living below the poverty line can't yield high taxable income. Guess that leaves the good ole middle class.... Yes, you and I, who pay for all of these things, politicians say are necessary or unnecessary. From the lower middle to the upper middle class, we carry more than 70% of this country's tax burden, yet it's not us that decides where tax dollars go. The lobbyist, big business and politicians make the decisions where the money goes.

Again, how ridiculous is it that we allow the people who don't pay their fair share of taxes, as the 5% group decides what happens with the dollars the majority of people pay, who live at the median household income level? Then, we allow them to continue raising taxes, charging us even more? Crime doesn't go down, poverty doesn't go down, homelessness doesn't go down, infrastructure doesn't improve, healthcare goes up, products go up, and costs of services go up, all based on the decisions of those in a completely different tax bracket. Meanwhile, the country is almost always on the verge of another civil war or race war. To my colleague, I said…. "Friend, we are all fucking idiots."

You have to give credit where credit is due, regardless of how horrible it may be. Back since the founding fathers constructed documents for this republic to follow, the powerful knew that if you gave people someone to hate, someone to blame and someone to look down on, that distraction would allow you to consistently gain more power and wealth while they were focused elsewhere.

To convince someone with whom you have nothing in common in regard to upbringing, lifestyle, preferences, or anything to stand by you in the name of fear, hate, and the perception of being on the winning team has remained a reliable formula for those in power.

In the typical scenario, most winners receive a tangible prize at the end of a race; however, in this case, only the powerful get the prize while the have-nots stand there and smile, believing that they've won something…. They did not win anything; in truth, they paid for someone else's prize. Ultimately, the prize the so-called winners are left with is only hate and fear that yields nothing profitable. This country's history is based on this theory and examples like this since its inception.

True hate typically brings about a calculated genocide plan. This kind of hate makes it clear that a group of people will not be tolerated for profit or for anything else. Economics is not hate; it's using the tools of hate to be profitable on the backs of those who will embrace them or those who are victims of those tools. Economics does not subscribe to these extremes of hate simply because it is not profitable. Extreme hate causes revenues to be lost, and that can never be allowed to happen for too long. This, unfortunately, is also part of our history, which is often disguised in the rewriting of history and what events truly took place. Economics doesn't like to be reminded of its failures and losses in dollars, so we act like what really happened was something different.

HISTORY, TRUTH AND GUILT

The histories of most nations tend to be very complex things. These histories are compiled of proud moments as well as moments of regret and things to be ashamed of. In most cases, someone usually wants to edit out or redact the not-so-great moments, but that is not true history. True history is comprised of the actions of human beings, which means that, like us all, TRUE HISTORY IS FLAWED. The ability to own up to our flaws just as we do the greatness, is always the challenge. The inability to accept flaws in our society is also what stops CHANGE for the better from taking place.

This, unfortunately, will not be a journey down the lane of great accomplishments of this country, but rather several historical themes that have impacted the way people in this country live to this very day. Again, there are thousands of amazing things about this country and the individuals who have accomplished those feats. Honestly, those are *typically* not the things we find hidden from the history books. The only time amazing feats seem to disappear from history is when the contributions are from individuals whom those in power perceived as inferior, but that is another conversation.

Most Americans have a hard time grasping the fact that slavery for the African countryman began in this country in the early 1600s. That means that we are looking at 410-420 years of severe to moderate variations of oppression to date. Unfortunately, the years grow beyond this time frame when looking at the plights of other groups, such as Native Americans; however, that is another complexity for another time. For decades, slavery was the primary driver to build this nation's economy. This labor force was one of the foundations that provided the path for this country to evolve into the superpower it has become. Tobacco, sugar cane, cotton, wheat, hay, textiles, farming land, raising livestock and more contributed to major economic success all over the country, with a heavier impact in the southern regions of the country. Generational wealth has been passed down from family to family due to the labor and deaths of slaves in this country. Without black people, many successful legacy families heralded as the cornerstones of the South simply wouldn't exist today.

Black slaves were treated as objects, property or working animals, but not like dogs or pets. Dogs or pets gained more respect and dignity than slaves did. The comprehensive breakdown of the black family and the emasculation of the black male were core elements in controlling this new property that plantation owners had obtained. Selling siblings, spouses, sons and daughters publicly served multifaceted purposes. Not only did it bring in revenue for the slave owner, it also crushed the family unit and kept slaves controlled by mentally breaking them down.

Often, the female slave was violated and raped in front of the family, with the husband unable to do anything about it. The male slave was often emasculated in front of his family and others to set the example of what happens when you don't comply. The purpose of these tactics was simply to strip all dignity and respect away from the male figure.

Behaviors like this proved effective in the control of uprisings on plantations. What was happening on a grand scale was the destruction of the black family unit. Over time, the black female became unable to see the male figure as the protector he once was. He was increasingly seen as a liability who was weak and wouldn't be around for long to be of any benefit to the family. Male fathers and sons began having to deal with the feelings of resentment towards females they witnessed being victimized day in and day out. From being assaulted, objectified and raped to bearing the children of the slave owners. Many female slaves were allowed access to the plantation houses, where work was not as difficult as in the fields. Outside of the plantation house, many male slaves watched women be violated by the slave owner in the presence of everyone. In due time, the female would adapt to the belief that life would be easier if the male simply weren't around. This would be less pain or problems for her and any family that was allowed to stay near her.

There are actual documented methods of torture as to how to keep one's slaves in line. These tortures were a mix of physical and mental duress that would either break an individual mentally or kill them. These theories and practices were shared and utilized by slave owners all over the country. Some of the methodologies and practices from this era are embedded in our judicial system and law enforcement protocols today.

While it is true that there were slaves in the north as well as the south, the south benefited an economic prosperity in this realm that could not be rivaled by the north.

This prosperity is ultimately what gave the South the ability to mount such a fight against the North in the Civil War. There is a phrase that says, "If you plan to go to war, make sure you have your money right", and the South definitely had that. It's just one shining example of how much economics is at the root of most things, even war. When it comes to economics, most successful people of all backgrounds tend to operate on the premise of conservative values. There are several reasons why post-emancipation, so many black people identified as republican, but one of the biggest reasons is, in fact, around economic conservatism.

Ultimately, power and economic growth made their way to the table between the North and the South. This is what brought the slavery topic to the forefront. While many people would like to believe that the atrocities committed against human beings are what started the civil war, it is not. As usual, it began around economics and later spiraled around the atrocities towards slaves, which then appealed to the more humane population of the North.

The battle of the political parties is very much at the heart of this civil war. Southern Democrats and Northern Republicans were clearly opposites of how they are today. Two factors contributed to that change, which are: Southern Democrats lost the Civil War, and then the PARTY SWITCH. You should look it up, but in a nutshell, the southern democrats switched to the Republican platform post-Civil War to chase the money after the loss. The northern Republicans did not welcome the southerners; therefore, they switched to the democratic platform, which had been vacated. Thus, the reason why in today's world, Republicans call democrats "bleeding heart liberals." This was the same thing the southern democrats felt about the north Republicans during the Civil War. When these Yankee Republicans began standing up for slaves, the wording wasn't bleeding heart liberals, it was more like "Nigger lovers" and brilliant phrases like that. In case you weren't sure what it means today when you hear people refer to anyone who stands up for another person's rights as "liberals, snowflakes", etc, don't worry, it's only that old Southern mentality telling you how they feel about anyone getting in the way of their superiority agenda. But I digress.... Again, the traditional conservative premise is based on the original Republicans who were in the North. This is why so many black people adopted those values once emancipation and the options of community building began. In fact, those conservative principles worked so well for free slaves that black communities began to thrive in many different parts of the country. Thrive means black banks, black schools, black business and entire self-sustaining ecosystems. For all intents and purposes, financial conservatism drove effective capitalism in the black community.

Unfortunately, time and time again, as these communities would prosper, white agitators would create fictitious circumstances to justify coming in to destroy, terrorize and kill those in the community who they felt had more and were more economically viable than they were. Tulsa, Oklahoma and Jacksonville, Florida, represent only two of many thriving communities that were completely destroyed by white invaders. The records of these incidents have been suppressed in history at the behest of POLICE departments and government agencies that were 20 times more openly brutal back then than they are now, if you can fathom that.

For the longest time, I must admit I didn't know much about the history of law enforcement other than my own history and experiences with police departments. While my experiences and those of my friends and family have their own validity, the nation's historic journey has implications on a national scale that are massive. An example of this would be in Boston during the early 1600s, when elected officials took the responsibility of being public servants for the people or those who upheld the law. There was no organized police force at this time. The first "organized police" entity originated in the South. This means that while up North, law enforcement was really a part-time responsibility taken on by perceived upstanding citizens to maintain some semblance of order, the South had already cultivated the ideology that law enforcement was only necessary for black people. The Carolinas created "slave patrols" during the 1600s, which ultimately became the model for the police forces that were officially formed in the late 1800s. Most of the men running slave patrols were slave owners or affiliates of slave owners who didn't see those they hunted as human beings, but as animals that could be treated any kind of way. This mindset of seeing black people as animals also became part of the foundation of policing and continues, by and large, to be a big part of the "threat" mentality that so many law enforcement officers have today. Things like this are at the root cause of black people being intimidated by the mere presence of police. These historic occurrences and more stem from the early developments of slavery up to the passing of the 13th Amendment and beyond. Because so many slaves ran to the north to escape, many slave patrols were very familiar with northern cities as they traveled to recover slaves and bring them back to the south, until before the Civil War.

It may sound ridiculous to those who don't know history, however factors like these and more contribute to why in this day and age the entire criminal justice system views black people as: automatically guilty, a threat to all society, so dangerous that an officer is justified in "shoot first ask later", liars no matter what they say, unpatriotic, un-American and not entitled to the rights real Americans have. Ask yourself, or better yet, go and research how slave patrols approached the job at hand, and you will see a glaring representation of today's legal system towards people of color.

As crazy as it may seem, because it happened so frequently, most communities never thought anything was wrong with the tactics of the brutal tracking down of slaves. In truth, these kinds of practices were documented for decades proudly. Hangings, burnings and quartering's were often documented as family events or community outings with kids running and playing around the mutilated, dead black bodies.

So…. imagine yourself on a slave patrol tracking those no-good, ungrateful SOBs that had the nerve to disobey and run away. You know that they are desperate, and if they even think of resisting when you catch up to them, you will teach them a lesson they will never forget. Keep in mind that some of these slaves are very strong and powerful, even if they don't realize it themselves. In fact, if they disrespect you or give you any grief, you will kill. You don't want to hear any excuses, lies or anything. They will do what they are told, take the beating and come back peacefully or in a box. You do need to be a bit careful tracking out of the south because they all look alike, and taking someone else's slave or mistaking your property for someone else's could cause issues with some of these sympathetic northerners. However, it really doesn't matter who they are because if they step out of line, they will pay. Black folks have no business thinking they can talk to whites the same as Americans can, especially to the patrol that has a legal right to apprehend them and anyone that looks like them. We are the law, and we can do whatever we feel is needed to handle these Negroes. Men, women, children, grandmas or grandpas don't make a bit of difference as they are all guilty of not wanting to bow down and be the property they are.

Sounds kind of crazy? It's not a movie script or a fictional vision; these are realities of how slave patrol mindsets influenced law enforcement approaches and policies once the 13th amendment allowed convicted felons to be enslaved again. After all, who would be the easiest to convict and place back in servitude? Who was the easiest to spot as a potential felon without knowing a name or identity? Who all looked like the new definition of "criminal"? In short order, much like being a slave, being a person of color was all that was needed for anyone to stand out to law enforcement. That was the criterion for automatic guilt to be arrested and placed into servitude. Today, I believe we call it "profiling".

Does this seem far-fetched to you? Does this seem out of touch with what happens today and how law enforcement views people of color? Ask yourself about the details of George Floyd, Freddi Gray, Tamir Rice, Jacob Blake, Sandra Bland, Casey Goodson Jr, Philando Castille and many others who encountered law enforcement. Look at the patterns, the things that triggered the officers. Review the behavior of the victims and the unnecessary force utilized time and time again by law enforcement out of anger, feelings of disrespect toward authority, profiling, intimidation and presumed guilt regardless of what the circumstances were. How far off are these current situations from what was happening in the late 1600s and early 1700s? The answer is beyond obvious, and while strides of improvement have been made on the backs of others who sacrificed themselves before us, we have such a long way to go.

The truth is, an educated person of color today can be more at risk with law enforcement than an obedient slave in the 1700s. Why? Because today we stand up for the same rights as other Americans do, and often law often sees that as a threat. "How dare you? Who do you think you are talking to? Who do you think you are?" This is one of the reasons why people of color who are parents must have “The Talk” with their children. An educated young black teen who doesn’t understand what he or she is up against when pulled over will find that the 1st amendment freedom of speech right can get your head blown off. This rule applies to male and female persons of color alike. This is not speculation; this is life experience firsthand. And no… not just my experience, but damn near every person of color that I know and have known for the last 50 years of my life. Some things are just not coincidences, especially when they coincide with a history that clearly continues to repeat itself.

This is not a condemnation of all police, any more than you can condemn all white people from the south or in this country as being racist. Absolute blame is as dangerous as racism, bigotry, or sexism because it can assume a platform that stereotypes all people in a group as the same. We all should know by now that in any group, there are always those that don’t buy in to a message, those on the fringe that take the message to far, those that aren’t 100% sure about the message and of course those that don’t care about the message but are along for the ride to get something for nothing if possible. No cause is ever absolute. Policeman, White nationalists, BLM, LGBTQ, Nation of Islam, Catholics, Christians, Muslims, Military serviceman, entertainment industry actors, Trump supporters, Democrats, Republicans, NRA members, Bloods, Crips, Vice Lords, Aryan brotherhood, Black Panther party and on and on all experience the same challenges with internal participants who march to a different drum then the organization does. What’s most amazing to me about this phenomenon that happens in every organization is how time and time again, the individuals who veer off the path are rarely recognized until major change is already in play.

History shows us that when groups in power bend and break the law in large numbers, they are given consideration as having "a few bad apples "or outliers in what is otherwise labeled a righteous movement or message. Groups that do not have power, that have the same scenario of people bending or breaking the law, find that suddenly the whole group and the message are marginalized as criminal and evil.

History also shows us that standards of ethics are not measured fairly towards groups with power versus groups without power. For example, crimes committed in the United States are prevalent in all races and ethnicities. When white individuals commit crimes against white individuals, they are simply listed as those who broke the law. When minorities commit crimes, the narrative changes to them being animals, those who destroy their own neighborhoods, brutalize their own kind and are the root cause of all that is wrong in this country. This narrative is typically reserved for the black and Latino community, more often than not, as if we break laws more than others.

Lastly, when Police officers break the law, instead of applying stronger accountability to a position with such authority, the comparison is made to people of color who are criminals who break the law and that accountability. As if it is not enough that an officer not only broke the law and betrayed an oath, the belief that this is an apples-to-apples comparison is insidious. Side note, the comparison of officers to white public citizens who break the law seems to almost never happen. How can you compare any average American citizen who is supposed to be brought to justice when they step out of line by law enforcement, to the individuals in law enforcement who have taken the oath and responsibility to do so?

The officer is not the same citizen as the criminal, even when the officer is a criminal. First, adults who have CHOSEN to take these positions know that it comes with greater power than a criminal or average citizen has. Because these positions have such power, they also come with expectations that are supposed to hold law enforcement to higher standards than average citizens morally and legally. Second, the legal DEMANDS that accompany these positions require an officer to effectively uphold and execute the policies and procedures of the law to the letter. Failure to do so can negate the crimes a citizen is accused of, but can also result in criminal charges against the officer for breaking those procedures, as that is also unlawful. If criminals truly had ethics, they would uphold the law the same as police officers, and we probably wouldn't have criminals, would we? That is not the way the world works, as everyone knows.

HOLD ON A MOMENT

I apologize……. Unfortunately, I am going to step off topic for a moment to deal with a situation that has just hit me today. Often, we are all faced with situations that test our willpower, faith and belief in many things. Honestly, that concept is at the core of what this whole conversation in this book is about. With all the ups and downs I have seen and experienced in this life, I thought that I was mentally prepared to shake off most anything that could happen that seemed or felt unfair. Oh boy…. was I wrong.

Remembering my grandfather (my mother's father) talking to me about his life and the things he endured is all I can feel right now. You see… my grandfather was an amazing golfer. When I say amazing, I don't just mean he was pretty good; I mean like Arnold Palmer amazing. The challenge for him was that after WW2, this country still didn't allow black men in country clubs unless they were serving, cleaning or caddying. It was very well known in our town that my grandfather had an extraordinary ability, and because he loved the game so much, he would go and caddy for members of a local country club just to be able to play. The doctors and lawyers who were members there would often let my grandfather take shots for them that would essentially lead to their victories on the course. After a while, there were two doctors whom he would consistently caddy for, and consequently, they were considered the best golfers in the country club. Imagine being considered the best-skilled person in a situation and getting rewards for being so when you know you are not? My grandfather never got the recognition publicly for his ability; however, one of those doctors helped to ensure that once black people were allowed to play the course, my grandfather could go anytime he wanted and never pay a dime. As nice a gesture as that was, nothing could ever take away the opportunities that he had been denied for decades simply because he didn't fit the mold of those in power. He would often tell me to do things because they make me happy, not because of what I could get from them. Later in life, I understood why he told me that. I realized the joy he received from the game, regardless of how he had been robbed of the fruit it would have produced for him had he been allowed to truly compete. My grandfather was once one of the strongest men I have ever known. This story is one of the easier challenges he dealt with in his life, which again speaks to his mental fortitude. He was able to accept that even though his ability exceeded those around him, he was still held back and not given a fair opportunity.

Today, a similar thing has happened to me regarding fair opportunity and has been tossed in my face just as bluntly as the reality that my grandfather couldn't play the course at the country club. Today, I found out that my skills and abilities couldn't hold a candle to someone else who simply “fit” the mold of those in power. Comparatively, looking at both of our skill sets, there is little comparison or competition, yet, much like my grandfather, I continue to take the back seat. It is not as if this is new for me, but it does seem to hit a bit harder today than in the past. Perhaps it’s the renewed awareness of our country’s climate, the content of this text, the reflection of the past and the conversations that molded me or all of the above, that make this weigh heavier on my person than before. We all know that life is not fair; we all know that, especially in business, people get screwed over. The ups, downs and disappointments of business are all too familiar to me, which is why it is easy to recognize the difference between things that are not business-related. That was also something my grandfather taught me. Just because he couldn’t get his due in society’s country clubs doesn’t mean he wasn’t a successful man. He was a son, brother, uncle, husband, father, grandfather, veteran, homeowner, respected man of his community and retired after 30 years with the same company successfully. He taught me that I also must get my due in other ways than what society may or may not grant me. However, that doesn’t mean that it doesn’t hurt when unfairness strikes.

At one point, I believed that the American dream was this: the most qualified person in the room or the best athlete in the room working the hardest wins. That is not true. The American dream is finding your own success in spite of the fact that the most qualified, hardest working or best in the room doesn’t win. These are the conversations I will continue to pass on to my own. But I digress…

ALRIGHT I'M DONE, LET’S GET BACK TO IT

One should question why it is so taboo to speak out against Law Enforcement or the authorities when something is wrong. For some reason, we as a people don't seem to realize that we can be and should be critical of something and still be supportive of it. Being critical of law enforcement doesn't make a person anti-law enforcement; it makes them a part of helping law enforcement to be better. Holding those accountable who make mistakes or break the law just because they represent the law doesn't make one anti-government. It seems that we have been brainwashed to believe that correcting issues or faults in a system is anti-American, but isn't that supposed to be the idea of growing to form a more perfect union? Can you name any business, organization or institution that did not have to grow and evolve by learning from its mistakes? Imagine if it never acknowledged its mistakes and refused to take constructive criticism and accountability to do so. Whether we like it or not, law enforcement and the legal system have a long way to go toward becoming as fair and just as they claim to be. In order to make those changes, input from all parties, including those who have fallen victim to its shortcomings, is necessary to implement true change. We don't seem to be ready to do that just yet. History is always laced with successes and failures in all societies; however, ignoring or denying the failures only hurts the future progress of that society.

Why would a society not acknowledge all the components of its history? Surely no one believes that any society only has success in its history and no failures, right? The United States is no different from any other country when it comes to its history. As the proclaimed leader of democracy and freedom in the world, you would think that we embrace all of our history and diverse makeup more than anyone else in the world, but we do not do that so well. Although we are clearly a very bold and proud country, those attributes are not the driving force behind why we hide our failures, in my opinion. My belief is that GUILT is what drives this country away from facing our failures historically, which continues to perpetuate our failures in modern-day history.

Americans are experts at claiming the greatest milestones of history as “we” and our achievements. From how we stood up against the British, screaming “the redcoats are coming!” to our role in WW1 and WW2. How we wrote the constitution, we made it through the great depression of 1920, medical, surgical breakthroughs in battling sicknesses & diseases, we dominate the world of professional basketball, football, and we have the most dominant military in the world. We were the first to walk on the moon, and we take pride in phrases such as “remember the Alamo!” and “Custer’s last stand”. The agricultural explosion from the late 1600s onward, building railroads across the country, the industrial revolution and the modernization of major metropolitan cities. We revel in what we now see as women’s rights, civil liberties for citizens, minorities in positions of power, and we celebrate the many religions outside of Christianity that thrive in the United States. In short, we as Americans do have much to celebrate and be proud of on so many levels historically.

However, as with any society, success does not come without sacrifice. Not all sacrifices are voluntary, nor are they fair and humane. Like most other countries, our successes have been forged on the backs of others, often in blood. At this point, “we” changes to “they” and what they, the ancestors, did, not us. Just as those successes carry a legacy a perpetuate continued benefits to this day, so do the lack of benefits from our country’s failures to those who were sacrificed for the masses to come out winners. That guilt is what everyone seeks to avoid accepting at all costs.

THE TALK

I believe it was Zig Ziglar who said, “You cannot solve a problem until you acknowledge that you have one and accept responsibility for solving it.” Unfortunately, this country does an amazing job at burying its head in the sand and avoiding facing its greatest problems. As a result, these problems are never resolved and never go away. The guilt of the sins of history often prevents a breakthrough for the future. Not to say that everyone simply suffers from historic guilt, because there are many who see nothing wrong with the horrors of the past. Those individuals are not the ones who should get our attention positively. The ones who don’t know how to handle the embarrassment of what was done and don’t know how to handle the guilt of positive benefits they receive from those actions to this day are the ones that should get our attention, for they are the ones that can help to solve the problems we refuse to acknowledge exist.

Slavery, Tipped Scales of Justice and Opportunity seem to be the biggest guilt carriers in this day and age that people want to avoid, ignore or act as though they are not true factors in the lives of everyday people to this day.

Almost every family has that dirty little secret that everyone knows, but no one ever talks about. Which really means it’s not a secret… It’s just dirty, and usually it’s not a little thing either. Welcome to slavery 101, America's dirty little secret, because that’s exactly what it is. While slavery is not solely an American attribute, the many subheadings that fall under it do tend to be our attributes alone. In many countries, slavery fell under categories like classism and caste systems; however, in the United States, it took many other forms that were much more dangerous. Racism, bigotry, supremacy, brutalization and inhumanity to specific groups of people took root to flourish in ways that had never been seen in other countries. When you look at places like Germany and

Australia, you can see that millions of aborigines were exterminated, as well as millions of Jews; however, in this country, we combined death and servitude together and then allowed it to grow and evolve. Our crimes against humanity in America didn't erupt and end within 5, 10 or 15 years, similar to other countries. No……ours continued over GENERATIONS. I would agree that this is a tough pill for anyone to swallow, which is why it is understandable how the guilt makes white America feel. Nonetheless, it is a real pill that does have to be consumed by those who have benefited from it if this nation plans to truly heal and change what we continue to repeat over and over.

By no means am I an expert on the history and specific accounts of the journey through the American slavery experience. However, I am an expert on the impacts of that journey I have seen and experienced, if that makes any sense at all. This is where so many in this country remain confused or cannot understand how ridiculously offensive it is when someone says things like "you were not slaves, so what are you complaining about?" When things like "Slavery happened so long ago that it has nothing to do with you!" This concept is similar to telling a woman that she wasn't born in the time when women weren't allowed to vote, couldn't hold certain jobs, were unable to speak out against abuse, not allowed to be more than just a homemaker, had no choice in deciding what medical care was best for her body and much more. All of those things impact most women now and are a huge part of the quiet struggle MOST females deal with every day still. How can a man truly understand the journey of a woman in this day and age? You would think his best option is to listen to her experiences in order to be a part of further solutions. To act as though the past has no bearing on the present is irresponsible and most often an action of avoidance.

The same is true for black people who attempt to explain how their current journey is riddled with parallels to slavery that were very much our origins in this country. No one can expect white America to know that journey; however, the expectation should be that our experiences are heard, deemed as valid, viable challenges in order to shape further solutions.

It was those in power who birthed slavery in the United States, and it will take those in power to strike down the remnants of it. The responsibility of true power requires accountability for all successes and failures, not just the things convenient to focus on.

How often has anyone in power openly accepted responsibilities for huge mistakes, horrors and cruelty to mankind they committed? We create isotope words or phrases that we believe provide shelter for those "necessary" decisions, such as COLLATERAL DAMAGE, NECESSARY EVILS and of course ULTIMATE SACRIFICE. All these words and concepts appear to be an attempt to shield those in power from the guilt that should go along with choices that hurt people and take lives. This by no means is a trait I am attributing solely to those in power. This is an attribute that the majority of people in this country have come to embrace and utilize as a deflection shield. We see it used by those who commit crimes, those who are unfaithful in relationships, those who lack business ethics, those caught being dishonest and a host of human behaviors that are wrong. So, avoiding guilt and responsibility is pretty normal in this day and age, as it has been for generations.

It is very interesting when one starts to compare how wrongs are corrected based on who the victims are. When we learned about WW2 in middle school and high school, very little was taught about the internment camps Japanese Americans were placed in during the war. Very little was covered about AMERICANS who were born and raised in this country being treated as the enemy simply because they had the culture of another country we were at conflict. Outside of the manipulation of education in schools of history, I was blown away by the fact that immigrants who came from other countries and stole this one from those that originated here would imprison citizens born here because they looked like someone from another country we had conflict with. When there was a conflict with Germany, a total of 11,507 German Americans were placed in camps like this. Quite different from the 120,000 Japanese who were sent to camps. One could ask why the disparity in numbers between the two involved in this scenario, but I will just leave that question for you to ponder and research.

More importantly, in regard to guilt, responsibility and comparisons, did you know how the United States attempted to make right the wrongs committed against those Japanese Americans? Legislation was implemented that stated "The United States government's actions were based on 'racial prejudice, war hysteria and a failure of political leadership." Ultimately, the government dispersed more than 1.6 billion dollars over a ten-year period (comparatively to the current economy) in reparations to over 82,000 families impacted by internment. While I do believe that was the right decision to make things right, I have a hard time understanding how racial prejudice can be acknowledged for those citizens who felt the impact over a period of only 3 years, versus acknowledgment for black Americans who have known nothing but racial torture since the early 1600s. It seems that providing apologies and taking responsibility for what has been done to black Americans is something that is not warranted for some reason.

One must wonder if that is just extreme guilt and avoidance, or does race and hatred enter into whether or not certain groups of people even deserve an apology from the government system that attempted to virtually exterminate them? Hatred, violence, anger and fear manifest their repercussions on human beings in so many different ways after the implementation of those feelings has taken place. For most people, the ability to face the repercussions of their actions is something that doesn't happen, which ultimately makes things worse for everyone. It means that we tend to perpetuate the behavior we already feel guilty for. It means that those victimized by that behavior continue to be victimized as the behavior is not stopped. It also means that the guilt becomes greater while forcing ourselves to swallow even more of what we are already full of. This is how people back themselves into corners they believe they cannot get out of, therefore committing to a lifestyle of horrendous behavior.

Lastly, and probably the most important when it comes to the guilt of one's continuous behavior, is the fear that if the tables turn, someone will do to you as you have done to them. Although it is an old cliché, we know that most people cannot handle receiving what it is they dish out to others. This fear often walks hand in hand with guilt. In fact, this fear often suppresses guilt, providing credence as to why it's ok to continue to act in such awful, unethical, immoral ways. The behavior becomes noted as "self-preservation" before it is done to you. Many who see equality in pay, justice, opportunities, relationships and human rights as a problem tend to believe that they lose something if anyone else has an equal shot.

Many see the equal shot as an uprising, to which the loss of power means that one day they will be unequal and less than everyone else.

THE TALK

If we are 100 percent honest, this is actually true based on history. Historically, nothing has been fair for anyone else not in power in the United States. The laws were not written for anyone other than those who looked like and represented the founding fathers. Therefore, any truth-up of equality does, in fact, take power away from those who have held it solely for 400 plus years. After all, who willingly gives up power and enjoys that? For a moment, it sounds like I am on the side of those who feel the guilt, fear and perpetuation of the racist oppression that has dominated this country, doesn't it? It's not that I am on their side; it's that I do understand power. I understand that to maintain power, tools are used by those in power to control everyone who is not. Those tools are racism, economics, bigotry, genderism, hate, political rhetoric, criminal justice systems, media and propaganda that create division and polarization.

This is all a game that is engineered and directed by the institutions in power. Believe it or not, you and I are the participants of the game. Revenue is created from our pain, suffering, death, success, promotions, evictions, terminations, births, weddings,

crimes, punishments, sicknesses, celebrations, consumptions and every other single thing we do. WE ARE THE GAME. We can't even see that our very existence has been completely monetized. It does have a nice title given to it called CAPITALISM, and we have been brainwashed to believe that anything economic label is a form of oppression equivalent to the dictatorship of Stalin and or Hitler.

Amazing how guilt can be used against people to manifest every other fear that halts the notion of doing the right thing or even being open to it.

In the grand scheme of this game, it's almost as if someone knew that this nation's guilt would be too great to conquer and change the wrongs to rights. Makes you wonder if, when the phrase "to make this a more perfect union" was created, it was said to excuse the fact that we won't get over the racial divide that keeps us from truly being a perfect union. That divide and all of the things that perpetuate it are what is at the heart of almost all that cripples the United States from being that perfect union.

It seems that for so long we have all embraced the role that we play, ensuring that this union never truly unites; we don't know how to play a different role. The carriers of guilt, the guilty, the careless.

THE ROLE WE PLAY

In the history of the United States, everyone who has laid eyes on this country played a role in its development from inception to where we are today. Some roles played were voluntary, while others were involuntarily and mandatory.

The evolution of the roles that each race, creed and color played in this country has been incredible in all aspects of that word. Incredibly amazing, incredibly sad, violent, prosperous, rejected, accepted, poor, sick, manipulated, criminal, strong, passionate, driven, family oriented, stubborn, educated, incarcerated, liberated, persistent, persecuted, brutalized, triumphant, innovative and on and on. One can add the word "incredibly" in front of any of the aforementioned adjectives, and it would accurately describe what people have experienced in this country. I don't know that anyone could have predicted how this nation would evolve once outside forces embarked on this land and its indigenous people. It makes me wonder if anything would have been different if the prediction had been visible.

The experiment in democracy, better known as the United States, has been one of the most successful horror stories the world has ever known.

How about that for an oxymoron phrase? The definition of the country envisioned when one mentions the "free world" is also accompanied by the realities of some of the worst atrocities committed against mankind by other human beings. In my experiences, I have often talked with immigrants who sacrificed everything possible to find a way to this country, only to find that it is very different from the propaganda they heard while in their own country. The reality of our truth here rarely caused anyone I spoke with to say that they don't want to stay here, as the opportunities still carry more weight than the horrible things that take place. Quite frankly, for many I talk to, this country still provides a sense of achievable stability better than places they came from. Ultimately, immigrants fall in love with the possibilities that "could be" more so than the dangers that are undeniably present. I suppose it's similar to black people who love living in a country that has demeaned, dehumanized and hated them since the 1600s. How do you love something that has seen you as less than human, bought and sold you as property, while not hesitating to brutalize, rape and murder you for generations? Yet this is the country we love and aspire to thrive, replicate and succeed in. That oxymoronic concept probably tops the list.

Sometimes, a person cannot see the forest for the trees until someone outside of the forest opens their eyes.

Being unable to see how you are being used and manipulated is a role that I think many white Americans have played and are still playing currently. I do not mean that in an insulting way by any means. For decades, I have watched black and white people live the same struggles, embrace the same fears and strive for the same success side by side. However, because the narrative has been perpetuated that nothing both races do is the same, white America, as a majority, doesn't see anything we all go through as the same. Crimes committed are not the same, death is not the same, success is not the same, being afraid, being a victim, suffering from illness, making mistakes is not the same, being naïve, being innocent and yes, being treated unfairly is not the same. The role white America plays has always been rooted in the foundation of acceptance, which allows entry into most everything in this country that most minorities simply don't have the same access to.

Through many, many fantastic relationships and conversations I have had with fellow Americans, I found that usually the things they took for granted as normal were things I had never experienced. The best part about that was that it showed how unintentional behaviors can be. I had a friend with me in my car when we were pulled over by the police. He was pissed… "You have done nothing wrong, and they have no right to pull you over! I'm going to tell them so when they get to the door!" His role was simple: right is right and wrong is wrong. It was his duty to address it. I told him to shut the F@!$ up, or he would get me killed. His role with law enforcement would be accepted, but the retribution for what he did would be projected… to me.

You see, he did not understand that the role I play is the receiver of unacceptance. He meant no harm, nor was he complicit in potentially causing bodily damage to me. My friend simply didn't understand the difference in the value the criminal justice system assigned him in especially compared to the value it assigned me. The shock on his face when I later explained that I had gotten upset, he would have been let go, and there is no telling what may have happened to me, showed me everything I needed to understand. I believe that most white Americans sit in the same space as my friend; we don't talk enough to understand it, so that those who are sincere, like my passenger, can truly understand and decide the role they want to have.

THE TALK

The first time my eyes were opened to the role black people in the U.S have according to the rest of the world, happened years ago while having a conversation with a man from Ghana. We were talking about countries and culture in general when he said something that really blew me away. He said, "When I think of black Americans, I always think about individuals who have Stockholm syndrome." If you think Stockholm syndrome is psychological babble, just open your eyes and look around.

For me, it was one of those moments like in cartoons or animation when a character's head goes nuclear, swells up and explodes.

Stockholm syndrome is a psychological response. It occurs when hostages or abuse victims bond with their captors or abusers. This psychological connection develops over the course of the days, weeks, months or even years of captivity or abuse.

His statement alone had ridiculous amounts of truth in it; however, I really wondered what meaning he saw in the statement. He had my full attention at this point. He was very clear that his thought was a generalized statement and clearly didn't apply to every black person in America. I appreciated the clarification. Though if I am honest, I was completely ignorant of how people from other countries viewed me.

Much like a person with Stockholm syndrome, black people ultimately accepted that the captor was and always would be in control. We had all but abandoned truly fighting back against the captor on a level that would change things. It often seemed that we would fight each other more violently than we would the captor. We had adopted the captors' way of life, rules and virtues as our own. Black people aspired to be like and acquire the kind of life the captors had. (Even though most of that success was acquired on the backs of immigrants who laid the foundation for that success) Black people lost track of where we came from and who we were before being taken by the captor. Before you go getting upset, this is not derogatory or a slam towards anyone. It is just the facts. Over enough time, anyone separated from the identify they once knew will eventually change shape to another identity.

Most importantly, when opportunities came time and time again for black people to change and truly be free, the ability to stand in solidarity to do so was sabotaged in one way or another. In essence, at times, the leash on our necks wasn't being held by anyone, and all we had to do was just take it off. Unfortunately, like any other creature on this planet. Repetition forms habits that are very hard to break. The repetition of being controlled and oppressed became a prison with no bars for a lot of people.

These thoughts hit me like a thousand bricks dropped from a third-story window.

Not only was the concept sad and overwhelming, but I saw all kinds of truth in it. Here was someone coming from a country that had all the things we were always told it didn't have, yet he knew the truth.

My friend knew he came from a land of kings and queens, a land where mankind began with sophisticated, intelligent societies. He was a product of a rich culture and history that which he was raised. A place where history books told the truth about people who were not natives, portrayed as naked savages with no common sense or modern ability. A country where, to this day, modern technology cannot replicate how the pyramids were built or create another system of mathematics, as Africa is known as the birthplace of mathematical sciences. It was explained to me that the problem is not that Africans don't like black Americans; the problem is that black Americans *in general* don't identify with Africans as much as they identify with their captors. Most Africans see this, and as a result, are perceived as not having a lot of respect for the plight of the black person in the United States. All I could say was……" well damn…."

Now let's be clear, we discussed things like South Africa, apartheid and the struggles that Africa has endured with outside forces trying to steal resources, take over the continent and yes, enslaved people there as well. They have also fallen victim, faltered and experienced some of what has happened in the U.S. The scenario always tends to be a bit different when you live on a continent where you are the majority. When you decide to wake up and rise, the numbers can be on your side. The reality is that no place is perfect or immune from strife or quests for power.

Ultimately, the more my friend and I spoke, the more it just seemed as though black Americans gave up the big fight and settled for trying to win smaller battles to be included in their captors' world. Kind of sucks when you get some perspective on how others look at things. Honestly, it made me think about the role we have played in the United States all these years. How the role began, how we changed it, the way we handled the push back against our change and how things evolved to now. It is impossible to act as though there have not been victories in the journey to seeking justice, equality and freedom. In the grand scheme of things, there are so many foundational changes that require much more fight. However, the fight must simultaneously include the things that black people need to change for ourselves within our own ranks. We cannot *only* claim victim status in this story. Some of our troubles are indeed "our troubles," just as any other race has. It just so happens that some of the other races can face their internal conflicts without the boot of oppression permanently planted on their necks.

Again, I am not an expert; I am not trying to speak for all black people in America and would never try to do so. All that I have to rely on are the experiences in this journey and my learned perspective. As we all have a perspective of some kind, we also all have the option of whether we decide to be honest with ourselves about what truth really is. Do we look at experiences in totality for what they are, or do we lean on fictitious perspectives that are selective of certain truths? Knowledge and awareness of the whole truth are imperative to understanding one's history and how things came to be. That truth and history don't absolve anyone from changing, improving and doing better.

This thought process allowed me to learn some truths of my own in our historic role played in America.

Dating back to the end of the 1400s, when Portuguese slave ships began trading Africans, the people taken rebelled and ran away from their captors. In the 1500s, when slave ships increased trading to Brazil and European countries, more and more slaves fought back against the "owners" who had purchased them and the work they were forced to execute. By the time the first slave ships made their way to North America, many Africans were very aware of what was in store for them if they survived the journey. As a result, there were many bloody revolts on slave ships from the 1500s to the 1800s, especially on ships that took the journey through the "middle passage" towards the Americas. Estimates of slaves that died on those journeys just through that passage range from five to seven million. It is estimated that one out of every fifteen deaths was a result of a ship rebellion. That equates to 300 years of fighting and rebelling consistently on all slave ships that made the journey on that route to the Americas. That's a lot of fighting for freedom before even having sight of the shores intended to enslave. That fight was part of the spirit of who black people were before landing in America and being systematically broken down. Upon arriving here, the process of stripping away that spirit, pride and culture of who we were became a relentless, nonstop endeavor.

The first role that we played was likened to that of a horse that had to be broken in to be trained for whatever use its master saw fit, until it had no use anymore. We all know what happens to a horse that is of no use anymore.... it is put down. Although, unfortunately, most horses lived better lives than the black kings and queens who survived the journey of the slave ships and arrived in America. Our role, like the most spirited, powerful horse one has ever seen, was simply to be broken.

Some of the tactics used to break the African civilians brought to America have implications and repercussions to this very day. It's important to understand that these tactics are why black people are still enslaved by the leash around the neck today. There are two tactics that stand out to me more than any others, having had a far-reaching impact. The tactic of separating and destroying the black family was first.

The second tactic was the dehumanization of black people to transition them to simply be seen as property.

Now I know this seems like trying to rub the past in the face of white people today, but it is not. It is the reality that I and many other black folks live with and experience today that needs to be shared.

In the beginning, slave owners immediately looked to establish dominance by selling sons and daughters away from their parents. Splitting up families that ultimately would have provided more value to the plantations they were on showed that breaking down slaves was the priority. Imagine being a father of a son or daughter and powerless to stop them from being taken away from you. In some cases, being made to verbally say that you agree with the sale just to further mentally break down the family. Imagine a wife, any wife, looking at her husband, unable to do anything as her children were taken and sold, never to be seen again. That trauma alone is enough to drive anyone insane and destroy any relationships. As slave owners saw the impact selling family members had on the male-female relationships of black people, the slave owners began center in on breaking down the father of the family. The way those black fathers felt being powerless to protect their own children was the beginning of what we see today in the absence of SOME fathers from the family unit. How many times have you seen the black father portrayed as absent in the media currently? This portrayal, regardless of how inaccurate it may or may not be, is prevalent in the news, movies, songs, and talk shows that we all consume. So much so that our society thinks it's an anomaly when they see a black man bonding with his son or daughter. How many schools, teachers, administrators, hospitals, and law enforcement agents automatically assume no father is present and are sincerely shocked when a black father shows up for his child? The narrative is still the norm in the twentieth century.

To further break down the image, the respect and paternal position of the black man, the slave owners also engaged in something called "buck breaking."

Buck breaking was something that slave owners did to males they believed were seen as powerful and influential in the slave community. They would gather everyone from the slave quarters to a central location and publicly discipline the black males for all to see. Often, the discipline would begin with beatings from whips or paddles until the male was bloody and exhausted. Once the man was exhausted, they would tie him down over a wood pile, table or bench and sodomize him publicly. The emasculation of the black man was an intentional act to destroy his role in the family or the community. Needless to say, these actions were truly effective as they achieved multi-layer impacts. There is no way that any wife, girlfriend, son, daughter or family member can view a father the same after witnessing that. There is no way a community can follow a man or maintain respect for him once they have witnessed such a thing happen. It all began with these kinds of acts over 450 years ago, while today the emasculation continues in different forms.

To top it all off, the men who were doing the hardest of labor in the fields with the strongest constitutions, men who rebelled, or tried to escape, often ended up being made examples of through beatings, hangings or sold away as livestock. These actions created an aura of abandonment for those family members and friends they left behind. Once this was established as a typical punishment, slave owners began raping black females regularly. Often demanding that husbands give permission to do so and ordering them to tell their wives what time to be available for sex. Again, imagine your husband coming to you and saying that the master expects you to be available after dinner to satisfy him sexually. To think that people wonder about the root cause of the conflict between the black man and black woman today….

It was simple: attack the children, attack the father, attack the mother, and you control the group as a whole by destroying the family unit. The methodology of breaking down and dehumanizing black people gained massive momentum from these early beginnings. Black people had no choice but to be engulfed in the role of being broken to obedience, brutality and servitude. The obedience of generations of ancestors is so ingrained in the black community that to this day, individuals will stand and observe law enforcement brutalize and kill someone in front of them with little to no rebellion.

How interesting it is that if one black person steps on another's shoe or feels disrespected even by a glance, there will be a fight or the killing of each other. The deep-seated fear of authority far supersedes our own solidarity or humanity towards each other. In other words, black people have become quick to attack their own as opposed to defending their own against the captor. In order to survive being broken, black people accepted that we were seen as property and not considered human beings by those who oversaw us. This was our next role after being broken…

The role of being property.

We often talk about the objectification of women and how offensive it is to not acknowledge her for all that she is inside, and not just the external look or the obsession. Think about what it feels like to not be seen as a human being or even a vital cog in the system that thrives and succeeds. For generations, it wasn't an option to be seen as an American citizen who deserves the same rights and freedoms as any other. Prior to the Civil War, black people were undoubtedly recognized as mere property or an asset for the better part of 265 years.

Playing the role of being property to someone else has far-reaching impacts well into the future of any race of individuals. After all of those years, the only way of life that one could possibly know is the one they have been exposed to by those in power. How one could not see themselves as an object is almost next to impossible, which has specifically prompted so many black people to accept the conditions and situations they find themselves in with minimal pushback to truly change that dynamic. In my opinion, one of the reasons so many people of color take some small bit of refuge engaging in jobs such as janitorial, cooking, hard labor, etc., is because those giving those jobs are much more amicable in seeing people of color doing them.

Funny, I notice that people are much more comfortable assuming that when they see me dressed in a suit at a business, I am in charge of security. That's a role that so many I have crossed paths with automatically assume they have. It seems that it's too uncomfortable to view me as a person of authority, knowledge and power. Although that statement may sound like an overreaching generalization, let me assure you that after 20 years of literally hearing the same comments in 4 different states, it's unfortunately very accurate. I have personally watched individuals become visibly physically uncomfortable with the fact that I am a leader in the career I have undertaken. The role that black people play as property or an asset versus being a crucial part of an organization has been ingrained into the fiber of this nation.

Being seen as property has been reinforced in the entertainment world for over 150 years, so that those who have never come in contact with people of color are guided to believe the images shown to them. Movies that only showed black people in certain roles that contained servitude or criminality, inflated the belief of inferiority and being dangerous. When you are seen as an object or property, the perception of you can be molded to be whatever those in power and the public at large want you to be. Truth simply does not matter because property doesn't have rights, property doesn't vote, doesn't feel pain, doesn't have feelings to be concerned about or human characteristics.

Property has a job to do or a specific purpose to perpetuate, and if it is not doing that, it is to be discarded. It's easier to kill or destroy anything that is simply seen as an object, not humane.

When something can no longer be controlled as an object or as property, what happens then? Historically, that something is suddenly LABLED as a threat and broadcast as such to everyone. How interesting that this very thing still happens to this very day?

The label of being a THREAT is probably the most heralded role black people have held outside the slave label role. Somehow, the South was able to elevate the perception of how dangerous and violent slaves were in order to justify the need to perpetuate captivity any time a conversation about freedom came into play. The goal was to hide the true angle of capitalism, free labor, terror and inhumane conditions while brainwashing society that these savages would eat your children and molest your wives.

No one ever stopped to ask why anyone would keep such savages working on their plantations for generations with such a huge risk of violence and death? Cotton pickers, field hands, those who cooked, cleaned and raised the kids of those who owned them for generations, all of a sudden became these vicious dark people who had to be restrained. The craziest part is that the label worked.... While the civil war changed slavery (which was more about the economy than humanity), the stereotype and generalization of the dangerous, violent black slave, now called a criminal, stuck like glue. We were simultaneously property people wanted to retain while also being a threat to the very society we helped build.

This role of the "big bad black man" is one that stuck, regardless of the behavior that he displayed. He could be as honest and wholesome as the next man; however, somehow, the "self-fulfilling prophecy" of criminality or violence always applied. Either way, we have never been able to shake the label of being more dangerous than any other people in the United States to this day. We were and are so dangerous, yet look at how long black people have been oppressed under the thumb of power. One would think that a group of people so vicious by now would have risen up and retaliated with a vengeance on a large scale against those who brutalized them. In actuality, the reverse of that concept has taken place for decades, and those who had every right to evoke vengeance with the utmost disdain and brutality towards the oppressors did not.

Confusing, isn't it?

Although many ex-slaves fought in the Civil War to contribute to the process of freedom from the South, most were not seeking revenge in the fight. Most simply wanted peace and an opportunity to live like decent human beings. There were many "all black" towns that began to thrive after the Civil War ended, doing exactly what people today say should be happening in many black communities across the country. These histories of these towns are not front and center in American history for several reasons, yet they did exist.

Towns where black people had churches, schools, stores, businesses, banks and agriculture. They had civil problems like any other place in society, but were able to maintain rules and decency.

Towns like Rosewood, FLA and Tulsa, OKL are but two of many examples of how black people were able to start anew, successfully and peacefully amongst themselves. Literally, the kinds of communities that the media harps on and berates us for not having now. What the media doesn't say is how town after town, community after community, were targeted and destroyed by those who did not like the success and growth of black people minding their own business. In many cases, it wasn't just towns being destroyed out of jealousy and hatred. It was the brutal massacre of men, women and children that manifested from that very hate and jealousy. The amount of death and destruction of black communities by white citizens from 1867 well into the 1920s is overwhelming. The black community was also part of the pilot program for mass killings in America, as were the indigenous people of this continent. The realization that 750,000 black people migrated to places as far south as Rosewood, all the way to Harlem post-Civil War, sheds a bit of light as to how vast many of these black communities were. It also speaks to how false the "dangerous threat" narrative about the black community was then. The real dangerous threat was the belief that life for black people could be anywhere near a comparison to those who had always been free.

Over time, it became evident that having a nice community simply wouldn't be allowed by those external forces. It also became evident what kinds of community those forces didn't bother? They didn't bother the slums, the poor areas or the areas that didn't have the resources to thrive the same way they did those successful communities. This actually became somewhat of a blueprint as to how to keep those forces away from many neighborhoods. It's a terrible thing that doing the right thing, living the right way, simply brought more death and destruction by those who hated black people. On the other hand, living the wrong way, embracing despair and crime, ultimately brought the same thing. A no-win situation was perpetuated. That is the other lesson black people learned in taking the role of the bad guy. By the 1920s, 1930s, much of the positive growth that had been forged started to shift in black communities, and those who had power over us for so long began to see the fruits of the horrible seeds they had sown.

The ghettos and the low economic areas we see today are nothing more than a reflection of the path black people were forced towards, as communities were attacked and resources cultivated from the ground up were stolen. Unfortunately, after years of inequality, many people of color began to buy into crime, violence and partaking in the same behaviors of those who dominated the country the same way for so long. When that transition began, the ownership of those actions also became solely our burden, and no longer was it on the shoulders of the captors that we learned from.

In this country, there is nothing out of the ordinary about bad guys. Bad men doing bad things is as American as can be. Though this is not something anyone wants to discuss, acknowledge or divulge, make no mistake that it is unequivocally true. Other countries sent their criminals and failed countrymen here, which is really how the United States of America was formed. Themes such as the "wild, wild west" were nice names for areas where bad men existed in lawlessness, disguised as something to aspire to. A society built on the premise that politicians legitimately steal money, power, and influence for themselves, the same as organized crime members or the mob did. The labels were nothing more than acceptable descriptions for men breaking any law established to get what they desire.

The rules of being a bad man change when color is introduced to the equation. One of the most accurate statements I have ever heard about crime when it comes to a black man came from someone on the television screen. He basically said that this country has always loved and respected a man who takes what he wants, as longs as that man doesn't look like a black man. Although this was clearly media, the truth in that media couldn't be more accurate. This country loves the bad guy as long as he fits into a specific mold. America was established under a criminal context and stolen from the beginning, so of course, much respect is paid to those who take what they want regardless of any rules. Rules and laws were made to control those who are not allowed to be takers. Rules and laws make examples out of those who do not stay in the place that was crafted out for them to be in. Most importantly, rules and laws were created by men who did horrible things to other men.

The law-breaking BLACK MAN. Sounds funny doesn't it? Or maybe it doesn't to you. Unfortunately, it is not a joke nor is it a parody of words. For generations, this is how all media outlets have reported on and portrayed black men, which is meant to instill hysteria amongst the public about this dangerous creature.

When a society already fears a group of people's differences both physically and mentally, adding some dangerous dialogue is all that is needed to ensure these labels stick permanently. Once the black man bought into these fears himself and began displaying the same negative behaviors of those who were in power, the deal was sealed. The oppressed is never allowed to function the same as the oppressor. That power belongs to the oppressor.

As early as the late 1600s, the fear rhetoric was used to capture runaway slaves by slave owners and slave patrols. It wouldn't matter if the runaways were nine-year-old boys; they would be described as dangerous men who would rape your wives and daughters, murder your family members and slaughter your chickens because they had no soul other than the blackness of their skin. Of course, it was never mentioned that these were children trying to escape being beaten, worked to death and treated worse than any livestock on a farm. You don't add humanity to what the world sees as a monster.

This rhetoric portrays the dangerous sex starved, aggressive, large and powerful black beast as something that to this day black men cannot get away from. White men, women and children were programmed to look down on and be terrified of black people long before they were free to actually commit crimes, so guess what happened when some black people decided to be criminals?

As one would imagine, a fictitious stereotype already in place gained major traction and became amplified thousands of times over. Not only was the stereotype seen as fact, it applied to each and every black person regardless of appearance, education or pedigree. All black people were dangerous menaces looking for their opportunity to hurt someone or get revenge for the atrocities bestowed upon them. How many of you reading this have locked your car door as soon as you saw a black person come near your area? Even though an individual could be in a white neighborhood that has the exact crime statistics as a black neighborhood, guess which one is deemed the dangerous neighborhood? The one that needs more police presence consistently. The one that everyone in the area is up to no good.

As laws were passed after the Emancipation Proclamation, creating a loophole to incarcerate recently freed slaves and put them right back on plantations, black people began to engage in "criminal" activity, not even knowing it. Suddenly, accusations of ridiculous violations and convictions gave way too many actually committing crimes. As so many people of color were falling victim to trumped-up charges, those who pushed back against this were immediately arrested for crimes like disturbing the peace, trespassing, etc. The trend of true criminality for black people began this way and evolved over time. *Thefts grew* to keep from starving, *murders grew* to defend oneself from those who would hang you or do you harm, *assaults increased while trying to* protect family from those who attacked them with intentions of harm.

In the beginning, all were crimes that started based on surviving a society in which black folks as citizens had no place.

Though the rules should not be different for those who commit crimes, the truth is that they are. Black folks who commit crimes already know that the penalties, sentencing and accountability will always be more severe than they should be or would be for other races. Nonetheless, that did not stop crime rates among black people from growing, nor would it be a true deterrent. Maybe if other facets of societal life were fair and equal, those legal penalties may have had a greater impact on correcting behavior. Ultimately, right or wrong, all people are responsible for their actions they take. No justification or root cause changes when a human being does harm to another human being. To act as though the things that black people have done wrong should not have repercussions is not true, nor is it what I am stating. Fair and just repercussions are what should be in place for everyone, just as fair and just opportunities to thrive in happiness should be as well.

That is not real life in America. Real life is violence, theft, drug use, addiction, poverty, murder and crimes that are as much a part of black neighborhoods as they are any other neighborhoods. Like every other race in this country, we kill our own, commit crimes against our own and do wrong to each other. It is a well-known fact that in any demographic, crimes thrive amongst people in close proximity to each other. In other words, all races tend to rob, kill and commit crimes more towards those close to them that they can reach. It is not the fact that we do these things to each other that is so appalling, or at least it shouldn't be. It is more the fact that after all that we have been through as people in this country, one hopes that hurting each other is the last thing we would do. You would think that watching others hang, tar, feather, lynch, amputate body parts, burn, rape and sell your own would ensure that we would never harm each other. Unfortunately, as flawed human beings, the atrocities we see do not stop us from doing so. In some cases, those very atrocities that we see create violently aggressive responses that have to be let out, regardless of who is victimized by the action. Crime has always been an act of proximity, no matter what the color is. Unfortunately, that concept is only discussed when certain demographics are on the table, typically not those of color.

Often times the conversation of "black on black crime" comes up. Typically, my first response is that "there is no such thing," which always shocks those in the conversation. How can something that all races and people do to each other only have a label when it comes to black people in America? In raw numbers, there are more whites in the United States than any other group; consequently there are more whites who kill whites, yet "white on white crime" is never uttered. FBI crime data shows a rolling trend that 80% of white Americans murdered die at the hands of other whites. 88% of blacks murdered die at the hands of other blacks. Both stats are staggering and unfortunate, but also relative. As a matter of fact, the civil war held 620,000 deaths, 2% of the country's population at the time, majority white males and still no label. Everyone knows that war was clearly more white people fighting white people than anything else.

For some reason, the United States has never labeled any other group of people with this narrative, not even the people in the Middle East who have been at war with each other at least as long as I have been alive. Have you ever heard "Iraqi on Iraqi crime", "Israelite on Israelite crime," and so on? We know that the Israelites and Palestinians do not get along, and they still don't get that label. The shocking look on people's faces when I share this data is almost always the same. People always say that they never thought about it that way. However, this narrative that is perpetuated still cannot and is not ever used to excuse the things that need to improve in the black community. This narrative is exposed simply to level the playing field in discussing solutions to our challenges in the community, just as other communities have their challenges.

There are many eras in the history of the black community that were impacted and influenced by crime. Clearly, there are some eras that had greater impact than others. WW1 post era kicked off an era of violence and crime in the black communities as many black men returned stateside from the military after years of digging ditches for the dead and racial humiliation from a government they were enlisted to serve. Black soldiers were paid less than white soldiers, thus making the return home a discovery of the inability to make a living on top of a host of other inequities. When faced with the obstacles of assimilating back into the community, many turned to crime to survive, utilizing many of the warfare tactics that surrounded them while enlisted. Drug abuse and mental duress had huge impacts on the behaviors of so many black soldiers as well as the families who dealt with them. Sons lost fathers, families lost providers, and men lost themselves, which brought about desperate measures on multiple layers. With minimal to no resources available to combat these obstacles, crime escalated and became another way to sustain financial, mental stability.

WW2 and the Vietnam conflict were very similar to each other regarding the kinds of impact they had on the black community and crime. These two conflicts did two major things to the black men around during these times. It removed many men from the community through the loss of life in war, along with drastically increasing the use of opioids in the black community in the wake of these wars. With the head of the family either dead or damaged from war, crime in these communities grew immensely during these eras. Spikes in prostitution, drug use, thefts, domestic violence, murder, drug selling, alcoholism and more ravage black communities, unlike ever before. From urban cities in the 1930s spiking in heroin use to most of the country turning on Vietnam vets coming home from what was deemed by many as a "lost war" that we never should have been involved in.

Again, with no help or resources from the government to provide support to the losses these communities incurred from a male patriarchal influence patriarch standpoint, people chose to take matters into their own hands illegally. Instead of social resources from the government, black communities received injections of poison by way of access to narcotics, subpar hospitals, poor medical care, insufficient grocery stores, substandard educational institutions, increased volumes of liquor stores on every corner, aggressive, abusive police presence and government agencies determined to undermine any unity or positive growth any groups attempted to implement.

The pursuit of economic sanctuary or mental escape drove crime rates to new heights year after year, destroying black communities and families consistently. We imploded many of our neighborhoods and saw that the only positive thing our crimes did was eliminate the need for those who destroyed the success of communities like Tulsa and Rosewood to do so again. These people were no longer jealous of the crime-ridden element we had evolved into when we had those communities. Perhaps that is where the "black on black crime" term came from after the country saw itself destroyed. It's said that the term showed up in the 1960s and in print from *The Chicago Daily* in 1968, as race riots had been underway behind police brutality. Who the fuck knows....

The largest crime impact on the black community really took hold during the Reagan era. This era for black people truly created some of the most influential thieves, pimps, prostitutes, murderers and drug dealers among us of our time. It inspired so many that have come since then to keep raising the crime bar regardless of who it destroys. All in the pursuit of money, power and fame in a way that the American system would allow. Better known as "The American Way."

Gangs and groups we recognize today negatively were originally formed to provide protection, education and resources to the black community. These organizations were changed to criminal organizations either by the label of the government or infiltration by impostors that ultimately contributed to making things worse for everyone. For some reason, the majority of black people could not see what was going on enough to do something about it prior to these organizations being corrupted. Bloods, Crips, Black Panthers, Nation of Islam, Organization of Afro-American Unity, SNCC, CORE and others all began with intentions of protecting and empowering black people through the extreme oppression unleashed upon them. Some of these groups lost their focus, were derailed, infiltrated, had top leaders assassinated or were converted to crime organizations with the help of external forces, but all had righteous beginnings with a shared purpose of improving life for people who looked like them.

Those who felt the need to survive by blending in, going along to get along and staying obedient to those who held power became internal weapons against these groups. This changed how we saw one another and held each other accountable for accepting wrongdoing against black people. It made it difficult to decipher who was genuine and who was a traitor. Often, the wrong people were accused of being saboteurs. While the external factors and influences have always been very powerful, it still boils down to what individuals decide to do, as there is no dodging accountability for one's actions.

Black people have always been a minority when it comes to access to power, resources, education and opportunities since their arrival in America. It's not uncommon for people to turn to crime when oppression takes place. This is not a characteristic specific to black people. In high school, I learned that this was the story of so many who came to America from Europe, already labeled as criminals.

Maybe we all have a little criminal inside of us that comes out if prodded or provoked?

It is truly amazing that black people are still here surviving through our own challenges, as well as the attempted annihilation by those who brought us here so long ago. No matter how guilty we are of crimes we have committed, the legacy we have survived thus far is one that NO OTHER GROUP OF PEOPLE CAN CLAIM. In fact, one could argue that black people committing crimes is not "our own self destruction" but simply manifestations of the society's imperfections, we live in, the same as any other group of people. Our manifestations are merely different based on the overall journey we have come through.

Oddly enough, the imperfections black people seem to show the most tend to be the ones that this country has labeled us guilty of. Or maybe it's just specific imperfections that are focused on in media of all kinds. A self-fulfilling prophecy is, without a doubt, a real thing. According to 2018 FBI data, there were 10,310,960 arrests for all crimes, ranging from Murder to even curfew violations. Black people represented 27% of those arrest. This number also means that 6% of the black population was arrested in 2018. That's a big number. Conversely, white people represented 69% of those total arrests in 2018, which means that 3% of the white population was arrested that year. Compared to the population per capita, black people had 3% more the number of arrests in the same year. This is where the media finds data manipulation justification in continuing propaganda that black people are the most dangerous threat, and everyone should fear for their safety.

The part conveniently left out is the other government data that states that black people are FIVE TIMES MORE LIKELY TO BE ARRESTED than white people simply because of systemic police practices. In other words, if we were all policed the same with all things being equal, that 27% arrest rate for black people would come down five times, or the 69% arrest rate for white people would increase five times. One or the other would change based on the true police practices. This is without addressing the fact that wrongful convictions amongst black people rank in the realm of 50%. So, FIVE TIMES MORE LIKELY TO BE ARRESTED AND OVER HALF OF ALL CONVICTIONS ARE WRONG. However, all things are not equal; black people know this still engaging in crime, fully aware that the chances of getting caught are always five times greater. Can't blame anyone else for that, but survival is survival. When risk vs reward is often life or death, feast or famine, one does what is needed to get their back from against the wall. This is not a justification; it is reality. Black people have been primed to play the role of the criminal for hundreds of years, ultimately ending up doing so more out of necessity than anything else.

You would think that a group of people who have been seen as this larger-than-life boogey man could never have been trusted to plow fields, tend to livestock, cook someone's meals, raise others' children, clean homes, be trusted with personal items in private spaces, etc. Yet somehow black people were simultaneously the most dangerous people as well as the subordinate, weak, humble and clearly trustworthy people to serve those in power. When I think about data, statistics and how information has been and is manipulated to demonize groups of people, it's mind-blowing. What's crazier is how easily the public just believes what they are told about data without thinking with their own brain. One of the comments I have been told time and time again is that "14% of the population is responsible for 50% of the crime in the country." Also, that 14% percent of the country is the reason welfare and government assistance programs are such a financial strain on the economy. Mathematically, do you realize how insane that sounds? Especially when the math is 42 million black people and 232 million white people. Basic math states that for every 1 million black people, there are 5 million white people. Is it physically possible for black people to use it that many financial resources in government assistance? Is it physically possible to commit that much crime at 14% of the population? Even if every black person in the country were a criminal? The question really is about if the data is based on the volume of population or per capita comparison. The volume of the population does not paint the picture that is publicized. Population volume clearly dictates who commits the most crime, who uses the most resources and should indicate a fair picture of the justice system. However, it does not. The data is manipulated using per capita comparisons against a group's volume and then advertised as a national impact on the entire country. Sounds confusing, right? Here is an example of how this works. 10 people are wearing red shoes, 5 of those people rob a store and get arrested. 50% of the red shoe wearers are criminals. Now, 50 people are wearing blue shoes, 15 of those people rob a store and get arrested. 30% of the blue shoe wearers are criminals. The headlines say "Red shoe wearers commit 50% of the thefts in the country. Now the country is looking at the red shoe-wearing people as the big problem that needs to be resolved. Sounds insane, doesn't it? Many of us subscribe to this insanity every day and don't even realize it. Those who are aware of what is happening feel as though they are crazy when engaging with those who either don't know what is happening or refuse to acknowledge it. Logic goes out of the window when it's time to justify brutality and injustice. I can't tell you how many times I have engaged with college-educated individuals who refuse to step into truth, logic and transparency. The preference to perpetuate and live a lie is overwhelmingly often the choice of those I have spoken to. It can drive a person insane trying to escape a label that is supported by fictitious numbers and data.

Above all, the greatest detrimental role given to black people to control them is that of being the inferior race. Of all the labels to hang around someone's neck, this one is the most powerful. You might say that imposing a death sentence is the most powerful label those in control can dictate upon another person; however, one always has choices as to how their journey ultimately ends. The ability to stand and fight back, be it to the death or for the right to life, is not an attribute of the inferior. Black people are still here in the face of all of these roles. Regardless of all that black people have endured through the journey of North America, the strength of survival has not been enough to remove the stigma of "inferiority" that remains, which leads me to believe that the label is not one that stems from truth, but from fear. The fear that, given the same opportunities, we can thrive and succeed the same as or better than those in power. The fear that violence, aggression, along hatred cannot prevail against civility, determination and passion. The fear that barbarism eventually succumbs to intelligence. The fear that vengeance for all the atrocities committed upon others will return tenfold if the tables were to turn.

To me, the fears of those in power are the things that have always bonded people of all races in chains. Fears that manifest from greed then escalate due to guilt, ultimately trapping all in a relentless cycle. This part is the story of the world, not just the story of oppression in the United States.

Just for a moment, can you imagine existing in a space where no matter what you achieve, others see you as inferior? How do you react when a homeless person without a pot to piss in walks by you in your business attire and says "stupid nigger" with confidence? What could possibly give a person with nothing the confidence to insult another person doing better than they are after evaluating their skin color? I can't tell you how often I have asked this question of myself, even though the answer is clear. A reality that I and many other black people know to be true is this, "The lowest white man would not trade places with the most successful black man, no matter what." When I heard Chris Rock and Dave Chappelle say this in comedy routines, it was funny as they used themselves as examples. They were also dead serious and fully aware that even with all of their successes, this was the truth. It's not so funny when the comedy show is over. More so, not so funny when you are not as successful as people like them. Accepting the reality that I and other black people are not looked at the same when we do the exact same thing as other races often further ingrains the inferior complex. When I was a kid, throwing rocks at cars, playing cops and robbers with toy guns or doing stupid pranks were not looked at as just boys being boys. You know, the way it is for white young men.

For me and my friends, it was seen as early behavior of a criminal or menace to society. Law enforcement needed to be present so that we could be taught lessons and get a hold of ourselves before "ending up in jail." Don't let me or my friends get caught toilet papering a house or spray painting anything, as that was called destruction of property, which required juvenile detention time and court cases for parents to be sued. Meanwhile, white kids would do the very same thing, and parents would work it out without law enforcement pressing for justice, stating that "they are just kids doing things that kids do." Do you have any idea how this and things like this felt witnessing my white friends experience such a different reality? This creates a psychological syndrome so embedded in your psyche that you don't realize the inferior complex being forced down your throat. The examples nowadays are literally the same as the horrific ones that existed when I was a kid. Ask Tamir Rice's family about how much worse it can get as just one example. Can you imagine a 12-year-old little white Johnny in suburbia shot and killed by police because he was playing with a toy gun his dad bought him from Walmart in his own backyard? How would that investigation go for the police officer who was the shooter? It likely wouldn't be the same as what the Rice family experienced. You can guess who feels like less of a family, who feels like their lives don't matter, who feels inferior, who feels like an animal. Get upset with me if you like, but Black Lives Matter is the same as saying "we are not inferior, we are not any less human."

It's not about Marxism, socialism, communism, democrats or republicans, but simply about human lives that have been treated as less than human for 500 years in this country. In fact, the belief that black people are inferior is so strong that for the last 500 years, those in power actually documented the atrocities they committed against black people and then told them to "get over it, it's in the past," as remnants of those atrocities still transpire. When situations similar to Emmett Till still take place today, how can anyone just "get over it?" Anyone who thinks saying let the past go is enough to pacify black people has got to believe that they are dealing with some of the dumbest, most inferior folks on the planet to even try that. How about in the age of video, we are now told, "What you see is not really what you see?" Telling people who are witnessing brutality live and in person that what they saw happen is not really what they saw? Then, finding a way to make that defense stand in a court of law, even with video, to accomplish not guilty verdicts? Well damn....That is a justice system doing the same things it was created to do when it was conceived in 1776.

That's not stupidity or inferiority of any group of people; that's corruption and power winning over everything. When truth and facts don't matter because those in power want a different outcome, people are often rendered helpless, feeling worthless. What do human beings do when they feel all hope is lost? They make horrible decisions, right? Think about economic depressions when men have jumped off bridges, slaughtered fellow employees and killed their entire family over money.

Think about women dealing with hormones and post-partum depression after having babies who have drowned their kids, suffocated them, abandoned them on the sides of the roads, etc. Is it so unbelievable that after years of the same painful brutality, death and hurt, black people resort to rioting and looting cities because justice wasn't served? Not to say that rioting and looting are correct, nor to say that all people who participate in these acts are doing it for reasons of change. Let's be clear, there are always a small percentage of individuals who take advantage of moments for the benefit in every group of people on this planet. Typically, attention to people like this is shown when those in power do not agree with the agenda of a group overall. It's at this point that the power structure implements a controlling narrative utilized to destroy the objective of the organization and desensitize the true problem that exists. The power structure is very proficient in manipulating the actions of a few individuals to denigrate an entire movement. So often, when righteous leaders in the community step up to oppression, those in power will use these very people on the fringe of that leader's movement effectively against them. It has systematically worked effectively for decades, from Huey P Newton to Fred Hampton, Elijah Muhammad, the Nation of Islam, Malcolm

X and Martin Luther King. From Medgar Evers to Marcus Garvey, the ability to dilute the strength of the true message with a fictitious criminal threat, internal or external, has been the blueprint for crippling progress for the minority against the power structure.

One of the most successful plans of inferiority towards black people has been the elevation of the belief of worthlessness, helplessness, despair and non-value of our communities. Once a group subscribes to being inferior, one only needs to provide the tools that will allow that group to perpetuate that belief. Liquor stores, drugs, subpar nutrition with low-value grocery stores, and substandard education systems all represent things you see abundantly in low-income communities. Out of experience, I can tell you that I believed my value was less than the other kids I went to school with. A big eye opener came after seeing where they lived and how it wasn't like my area, their schools did not look like schools where I lived, shopping and grocery stores were nothing like the mom-and-pop corner stores around my way. Those things alone had an external psychological impact on me before one word was spoken. When the playing field is not level, someone is going to feel like the lesser performer, regardless of the truth. While some do stand up and fight to successfully overcome the obstacles of the field, this does not mean that the field has been fixed. It's extremely frustrating when those who fight through the obstacles are then used to make everyone else look inferior or lazy because everyone else didn't make it. Pointing at a few who are rich, successful, educated, cultured or even presidential does not and cannot truly convey the meaning that "if they can do it, anyone can." Those rules don't apply in any other circumstance of normal society, so why should they be applied to black people who have historically been under the boot of multiple systems for generations?

Is everyone in corporate America a manager, supervisor, or leader? How about all the college athletes who are golfers or swimmers? Do they all go on to the Olympics or the PGA? Do they feel like they are less of a person because they don't go on to do those things? How about blue-collar workers who have careers in fields such as oil rigging that make great money a regular workers? Everyone on that rig is not a supervisor, foreman or manager, yet they don't feel left behind because of that. There are two common themes here, with the first being that as long as one can have pride in what you can accomplish, it doesn't matter if you are not at the top or in charge of everything. The second theme is that others are not made to feel less than because they are not super rich, leaders, supervisors, managers or those who run operations. Others are allowed to have pride in whatever they do and not be looked down on for doing it. Historically, in this country, the factory worker, the shipyard worker, carpenter, auto mechanic, HVAC repair, plumber, etc., were all considered jobs that were the backbone of America. No white male would feel "less than" for selecting careers in fields like this. Granted, these weren't jobs of the wealthy, but they were labeled as jobs that provided "an honest day's work" and were enough to take care of a family. Black people weren't traditionally allowed into these types of jobs for generations;

therefore, Janitorial, housekeeping, cooking, field work and farming were the jobs determined applicable to us. Minimal pay was provided at best, and at no point was the label of an "honest" day's work associate with these options that black people faced in this environment. More like backbreaking slave labor for pennies on the dollar. Hard to feel good about killing yourself at work as a provider.

In order for black people to not feel less than about not achieving the status of the few superstars such as LeBron James, Jay-Z, Beyoncé, Robert Johnson, Barack Obama or Will Smith, the playing field would have had to have been fair and level so that access to making a "decent" living was an available norm. This alone is what allows a person to be proud of whatever profession they seek out to achieve, short of being a millionaire. Again, the reality is that most white people who live "average" lives would love to have the wealth of the black celebrities listed, but overwhelmingly would not want to trade places with their lives if it required dwelling in that black skin. They are perfectly content with the "decent" life they have always had access to.

It's got to be amazing to feel that being broke and homeless is still not enough to change places with another person if it meant giving up being white. Like it or not, there is a certain security in being part of the dominant majority in power. Clearly, it cannot be said that "all" white people feel this way, but you get the point. In a nation that has more than 265 million white citizens, recent election voting percentages give a pretty good indication of the directions people wanted things to go and how passionate they felt about it.

Inferiority narratives directed towards minorities, perpetuated by our founding principles and legal systems that run this country, are very real. This is not said out of anger or retribution towards anyone or anything, but rather the raw, truthful acknowledgement of what must be accepted as reality before it can be changed. We as people are so busy trying to overcome the system one way or the other that correcting it continues to be lost, generation after generation.

Often, we fail to see or acknowledge the root cause of issues that we engage in battle with using our hearts and souls, simply because the battle is what appears to be most important. One's drive, desire, passion, dedication and other tools utilized can drown out those obstacles that shouldn't exist when the playing field is level. When we lose sight of the uneven playing field, we start questioning why a person doesn't have enough of these characteristics to succeed. We start asking why a person would rather "play the victim" as opposed to simply overcoming the obstacles in front of them. Often, the truth is that a person is not "playing" the victim; they have lost the regular game on the uneven playing field, trying to have a regular life.

As I have been told repeatedly by others, not everyone doesn't wants to be a leader; some just want to go to work and go home. Black people should feel that they can do the same, provide for their families and have peace in just being average. Unfortunately, many black people are required to be ten times better than the qualifications of even that "average" job just to get a shot at participating and being ten times better still doesn't solidify one's chances. You can see how an inferiority complex could set in many different ways, whether one is ten times better or not.

Throughout the history of the world, many different groups of people have been brutalized, enslaved, slaughtered and in some cases, almost completely annihilated from existence. Many other groups worldwide have also been labeled and stereotyped just as black people have; there is no doubt about that.

To speak on the stories of those groups, how they feel and what they endured historically and to this day is not something I can do. The difference that I see is that often the desire to listen and empathize with those groups is present among people of color. From women's rights to the LGBTQ community, comfort is found in aligning with those who have often been identified as one of the most oppressed people in this country for over 450 years. Even the most recent arguments about DEI and affirmative action seem insane to me. The largest benefactors and recipients of both acts are not the black citizens. It is and has been the white female, as she has been restricted from almost as many opportunities as the black American over history. As a result, she has gained more access and freedoms through the fight shouldered by black people.

Again, everything we consider does not have to be a binary choice and highlighting what black people go through and feel does not discount any other group's experience. It doesn't have to be "black people's" struggle or no struggle at all. It doesn't mean that other lives don't matter when I say black lives matter. However, everyone should receive **their moment in time** for resolution, especially when those responsible don't do what they should to remedy those conditions they created. Making things better and fixing wrongs committed has been the way for many other groups and races in this country. It should be the same for Black Americans as well, but it is not. The more time continues to pass without equal resolution, the more it confirms that this country simply doesn't believe black people have value the same as everyone else does. I don't know about you, but not acknowledging the truth of a black individual's journey makes me feel like I am less of a citizen or human being than everyone else. That is a hell of a weight to carry while trying to live a successful existence and perpetuate being the "model citizen America claims it expects me to be.

Nevertheless, millions of black people, along with millions more Americans who unite with black people through the struggle, continue to press on because love is ultimately stronger than hate.

The spirit of life is not easily broken and has proven to be never-ending.

OUR TRUE HUMAN SPIRIT REMAINS

One of the best things any of us can encounter in this experience is how magnificent the human spirit can be. With all of the horrific things we are faced with in life, we often don't give enough credence to the other side of the coin that balances tragedy. The beauty of humanity transcends economics, race, creed and color when we allow it to show itself to us. Many refuse to believe this notion or can't see the beauty the human spirit can represent when competing with all of the external noise of this life. One cannot appreciate the good moments in life if they never endure the bad moments in life. To do so means that one needs to acknowledge truthfully the good and the bad that exist in the society we live in. The inability to know the difference between right and wrong or simply to accept those differences can often be huge obstacles in seeing the beauty of the human spirit.

Love versus hate, Truth versus lies, enemies versus allies, peace versus violence, honor versus envy and fear versus acceptance are all differences that drive and divide us. The components of human conflicts, such as these, play major roles in the actions we take toward each other daily in the journey of life.

When I reflect on how many people were genuinely mortified watching the death of George Floyd shown on television for all to see, it shows me something. It showed me something when millions of citizens of all complexions mobilized together to actively protest against what they saw and committed to speaking out against brutality. It showed me how tragedy can spark the beauty of humanity in the darkest of moments.

This is clearly not something that happens every day. Just do some research in documented American history alone, and it will tell you this. Certain tragedies simply do not have the same impact as others do, like it or not. George Floyd is not the first person to be brutally murdered or publicized for the world to see as it happens. We have seen video footage of countless citizens killed unnecessarily in the last few years, and it did not move all walks of life the way the situation with Mr. Floyd did. The number of videos I have personally watched via the news or social media of black folks losing their lives for not committing a crime is far too many. While cases like that of Eric Garner, Philando Castille, Ahmaud Arbery, Andre Hill, Laquan McDonald, Rayshard Brooks, Breonna Taylor, Stephon Clark, and so many more caused outrage in the community, they did not spark the same volume of response as Mr. Floyd's situation. It made me wonder why?

Truth is, I have no idea what the difference was. Many believe that with COVID-19 impacting so many people to be at home away from the distractions day to day life, this moment commanded the attention of damn near EVERYBODY. There were no distractions to allow us to look away or bury our heads in the sand this time. Historically, there has always been something else to contend with or band-aid the horrible things that people endure around brutality. Maybe this was the variable with George Floyd, maybe not?

THE TALK

In looking at incidents that took place years prior to the Civil War, some of the same atrocities that had been common practice in the southern states suddenly became more and more unacceptable to those who had turned a blind eye for quite some time. Those in the north who were resolved to "mind their own business" and had been that way for decades were now involved in a crusade to change the depravity and torture of black people entangled in slavery. In other words, during some of the darkest times documented in this country, it was a commonplace practice for those who suffered long before it was documented as a problem. The good thing is that others finally found power in their own humanity to shine the light and fight. Regardless of what the true motivation behind the spark of change that brought about the civil war was, the benefit that change brought is pertinent. Much like those before George Floyd, unarmed black men, women and children of color being killed was no more a new occurrence than slavery horrors were prior to the Civil War. People in this country were very well aware of what slavery was, just as many citizens were very well aware of the concerns of police brutality in the black community. For some reason, it seems that historically, the human spirit always reacts to a spark before it truly rises to show its strength and beauty, doing the right thing. Be it the world fighting off Hitler and his quest for domination after watching it gain momentum, be it abolitionists fighting for the rights of people enslaved or rebels standing against regimes in the Middle East waging warfare on their own citizens, there is always a spark different from previous incidents that provokes the human spirit to rise up and fight for humanity. It seems that even in the world of what we call crime, the same principles exist. Visit a prison filled with individuals convicted of criminal acts and have witnessed all kinds of things deemed criminal. You will find that certain crimes or even accusations of those types of crimes are not tolerated by those who inhabit the very walls of said prison. Child molesters, those who murder innocents, rapists, etc., who enter the prison system are known to face consequences from other inmates much more severe than a sentence from a judge. This example just goes to show that the human spirit is not always "justified" or wholesome in its response, but it is said that beauty is often in the eyes of the beholder, right? So be it….

Through generations, we have seen the human spirit rise in conflict on behalf of women's rights, child labor laws, domestic abuse, and drunk driving. Homelessness, starvation, drug abuse, eating disorders, bullying, mentoring leadership of the youth, music, art, fashion, and so many other things that showcase how wonderful we can be to each other and ourselves in times of turmoil. Do you remember the young man who climbed the balconies to save a child falling in Paris? Or the group of people who bonded together as a human chain to save a family of five in Pennsylvania from flood waters overtaking their car? How about the ultimate sacrifice, where a 29-year-old Sikh man died trying to save three children in rushing waters that he didn't know? His actions ultimately caused him to drown in a California river in hopes of saving the lives of others.

Every story of the human spirit rising to a challenge doesn't have to be a tragedy. The situation with the black Principal at a middle school in Indiana comes to mind. The principal was faced with a student acting out in class, disobeying his teacher. Instead of jumping to negative conclusions or reacting from an authoritative perspective, he responded as a person, parent and listener. He was able to find out that this pre-teen was not comfortable with his haircut and simply wanted to feel better about himself. This adult, who just happened to bear responsibility for children at this institution, asked the young man if he would allow him to fix his haircut so that he could go back to class with confidence and no problems. The young man agreed, the principal went home to get his clippers and returned to give him the haircut he was happy with. No suspensions, no police called and no more problems. We don't know how much impact this will have in the future on this young man's life, but we do know that the day this happened changed his life from a negative situation it could have been. For me, this story speaks to so much more than just the human spirit. It speaks to how much it matters to have representation and familiarity. To understand what it means as a young man if you're your fade isn't right, or your line is crooked on your cut, is not something that everyone can understand. We all need to see people who look like us, communicate like us and feel what we feel in order to help us grow. We also need people who are different from us so that we can expand our knowledge and admire other qualities of human beings. Diversity truly makes us all better when we embrace it. There are countless stories like this that make your heart swell with joy. Ultimately, it seems like the gift and the curse that we as human beings carry within our being. The ability to be vile monsters committing acts of inconceivable horrors, simultaneously capable of being the most loving, compassionate, self-sacrificing individuals for our fellow human beings.

It has taken a lot of reflection and learning for me to even begin to scratch the surface of what it means to exist in this skin on this journey. Quite frankly, it seems that human beings are both the best and the worst at how we treat each other, along with the things around us. Those appear to be our two main attributes. There is no exception in any race, creed or color where these duo elements don't exist. While historically there are some groups of people that exude a higher level of aggression, violence and barbarism, the ultimate leader of these negatives tends to fall on those groups who wield the most power. These groups also tend to be the ones who create distractions that influence individuals to misplace accountability, abandon humanity, justify brutality and place the responsibility of harm at the feet of those victimized by power. A wise man once said Powerful entities will have you hating the people that are oppressed and loving the people doing the oppressing." We are often led to believe that the worst of us in a society mainly exists in the plane of the low economic criminal world. Other than the negative connotation that lawyers get, society assumes the individuals in certain professions are the best of us and couldn't conceivably be the worst of us. Be it doctors, Judges, law enforcement, scientists, CEOs, engineers, military, teachers, religious leaders or even Presidents, the perceived belief is that certain titles grant goodness as a quality in a person. This is not a fact, but more like a narrative used as a distraction. This is not to say that there are not amazing human beings in these high-level professions and many others! There are selfless acts of heroism, care and sacrifice that human beings in these roles display daily. The ability to recognize authenticity in the things we do and not allow the manipulation of humanity's beauty is the challenge we all face.

There is a saying that "people become the environment they surround themselves with." The influences around a person have a profound impact on the choices they make and how they see the world they live in. What would happen to us if every time we turn on the news, pick up a paper or read a social media post, it was more about someone who saved a life, helped a person across the street, stopped to help change a tire, diffuse a conflict, stood up for someone being bullied, praised another's accomplishments, intervened in someone's depression, gave an opportunity to a less fortunate person, showcased 20 newborn baby births a day and on and on? Would we be a better society if we saw a better narrative? I often wonder what impact things like this would have on the country. This is not to imply that bad things don't happen; of course, they do. The truth of bad things happening is realized simply by living in the moment. This is one of the reasons I believe many people avoid the news, stating that it is almost always stories that are depressing. What happens when those moments are actually used as a tool to create negative perceptions in an environment? News outlets choose to report on 20 heartbreaking stories every hour, mixed in with two "feel-good" stories that run every 4 hours on that day. These entities know that tragedy, theft, murder, backstabbing and conflict draw more attention than the warmer side of humanity. For some reason, we just can't turn away from indulging in the worst things about our nature. Humanity has been manipulated to be drawn to darkness more often than to the light for some reason. We are programmed to expect the worst, become desensitized in the face of it and continue to wait for it to repeat. Those in power have used this dynamic publicly as a tool for generations.

If we all witnessed positive norms consistently, would it perpetuate different behaviors in us, the same as the negative norms have? The positive lessons are not new or complicated. When a child is raised to be respectful, caring and

thoughtful in an environment that operates that way, this is often what the child grows into being as an adult. The same applies to education in the environment, religion, economics, literature and yes, love and kindness. Holding doors for people, saying thank you and saying excuse me are all habits that we learn not just from being told to do so, but from watching those around us actually do it. Being examples of doing things like this not only impacts our children and their behaviors, but it also serves as a reminder to adults of how they should conduct themselves. Influence sits right at the core of the human condition. Influence is often the game-changer once we know and understand right from wrong. With the right amount of time, repetition and exposure, negative influence can convince a human being to go against what they know in their soul is right and do the wrong thing.

Distractions carry the same impact as influence does and are often the first weapon used to manipulate positivity. Distraction has always been a tool used by the powerful. For those who believe in some of the oldest stories told to man, beginning with Adam and Eve, also know that the serpent was the distraction to change the positive environment they had into something else. While this may sound cliché, this concept is used to this day in every facet of mankind's existence. Politics, entertainment, war, economics, government, you name it, the same tactic is used to gain leverage. Many partnerships and relationships fail due to distractions, in my opinion.

Earlier in this chapter, I mentioned how the death of George Floyd has such an impact on this society, in part because the pandemic had settled in, and most of the country was at home, tuned in to actual life. There were not enough distractions to keep the public at large from digesting or avoiding this heinous act. This was not a new occurrence to those who have been victimized for generations, but it was new to those who had been distracted by our societal systems for so long.. Look at what happened when the distractions were removed, and the veil was lifted. Humanity resurfaced in the form that it always has when the truth is revealed. Does this mean that all is well, and it's time to go back to burying our heads in the sand? Not at all, but it is a moment that we need to learn from and process the true power of distraction. The power of people prevails in the reduction of distractions. It's my hope that we can recognize the nature of the kind of people we are supposed to be in these lessons we learn, leaving behind or at least minimizing the kinds of monsters that we have been for so long.

Have you ever wondered why certain movies and movie soundtracks invoke that feeling inside of you when the good guy is about to succeed? How about when the underdog is about to become victorious or when the impossible quest has become possible? Do you wonder why that warm feeling you get inside grows when certain kinds of music play in the background of an emotional scene? Organizations have mastered how to tap into this beautiful human spirit we are speaking of. It's amazing how sometimes these feelings are tapped into in order to make us feel all warm and fuzzy about an underdog or even a villain of a story. Even though most villains in movies and stories don't start out inherently evil, if you aren't careful, you will find yourself feeling more empathy for the aggressor as opposed to the victims of that aggressor. I'm reminded of this kind of scenario at the end of the movie "The Black Panther". When the character Kilmonger is dying while sitting next to T'Challa, watching the Wakanda sunset, his father told him about it as a child. For those moments in that scene, you find yourself feeling warmth, love and empathy for Kilmonger. You want him to say that he would like to become a better person and fight for what's right if T'Challa saves him. Instead, he decides it's better to die than to remain incarcerated for being who he had worked so hard to become all his life. He was not willing to change from who he had become or the things he had done, no matter how bad they were. The audiences felt for him and wanted this man, who had been killing people on all seven continents, to leave his trauma behind and become one of the good guys. If we aren't careful, the manipulation of the human spirit can create misplaced empathy towards those who must face accountability for their actions. This happens in real life outside of Hollywood.

The fine line between being wrong and righteous can easily be blurred. Malcolm X once said that an irresponsible press will make the criminal look like he is the victim and make the victim look like he is the criminal. Unfortunately, we see this all too often in our society today in things like the following.

What the law determined as a crime of narcotics for participants in the 1980s was later seen as an addiction that requires medical attention and help for participants in the 2012 realm and on. In 1967, 30 armed black men attended an assembly in the Capitol's chamber in Sacramento to speak out against racist legislation. It was legal to have weapons in the chambers as long as they were not concealed. State police, for some reason, still confiscated the weapons, and the decision was made to detain all of the men to have them checked out. No one was injured, arrested or killed, and no laws were broken.

On January 6th of 2021, thousands of people descended upon the Capitol building in Washington, DC, in the midst of the joint session where Congress counts electoral votes for the President of the United States, where they would mount an insurrection that resulted in five people being killed and 138 police officers being injured. Out of an estimated 10,000 people who were at the capital, about 700 were arrested over a 9-month period, and 105 were federally charged. What are the differences? Do you know?

My grandparents used to say, "Sometimes you have to throw a rock, sometimes you have to hide the rock, but you always keep the rock in your hand." Does this apply to the individual who is the villain or victim? Who is the good person or the bad person? Are we talking justified self-defense or senseless bullying? The answer, unfortunately, is just YES. The same rock used by a man who terrorizes people can be picked up and used by a defender of the innocent to stop bad things from happening. The same rock that was used to inflict treacherous pain suddenly becomes a beautiful tool of humanity in another person's hands. These days, the question more and more is around the narrative of who is actually the bad guy? Our society often waits to be told what to believe and who the bad element is, instead of just observing the obvious answer for ourselves.

In the end, I do believe that the human spirit knows right from wrong, good from evil. Anytime it begins to feel to you as though human beings are so lost that we cannot rebound from the ditches we have created for ourselves, just spend some time with young kids. That will get you back in line with reality. Watching 3-, 4-, 5-, and 6-year-old kids play together is probably the truest reflection of what the spirit of human beings really is at its core. Kids are brutally honest, but rarely out of animosity or maliciousness. They don't know how to articulate all of the emotions they feel, but they don't hide them or subscribe to social norms. Children are fearless. They couldn't care less about skin color, weight, height, clothes or physical appearances. Yes, kids plainly state what they see when it comes to those characteristics, but all they really want is to play and have a good time with anyone who is around. They don't care about job status, salaries, family bloodlines, political affiliation or tax brackets. If you want to learn how to be a genuine human being, watch a 4-year-old around other kids. Some call it naiveté; I call it our origins. Life is often great with children until parents and the environment start imprinting their biases on them. "Don't play with him, he looks dirty. Her parents don't look like they have much. We don't associate with those people." We literally ruin the pure human spirit our kids carry when we do that crap, and we consistently do it. All because of our shortcomings as adults.

Yet somehow, through all of the impact of external forces, a piece of that beautiful spirit remains in us and can be summoned at times to stand up for what is right. It's always been amazing to me to think about the fact that the same things that give us power can also be the exact thing that is our downfall. Desire, ambition, passion, determination, creativity, loyalty, leadership, and dedication are historically qualities of the best and worst in humanity. The choice of how we use the human spirit has always been the thing that decides our fates. I believe this concept is why people in the United States love any story of an underdog. It's the belief that in spite of the worst circumstances or odds, the human spirit can find a way to still come back and be triumphant. The team that made it to the playoffs that wasn't ranked the season before, the student that nobody ever expected to graduate high school ending up at an Ivy League university, the fireman who runs into a burning building and comes out with a child that should not have still been alive, but was. We label things like this "feel-good stories," however, I don't believe that is what they are. These are situations that appeal to the best part of our human spirits. We have become too embarrassed to just acknowledge that joy and instead create labels to make it acceptable to embrace those feelings openly if you decide to show them.

The most recent example of the beauty of the human spirit showing itself for me is a situation similar to the ones that have recurred multiple times in the history of this country. I'm reminded of 1861- 1865 when the country split in civil war, and yet so many stood for what was right. Then, in 1883 when the courts ruled that the Civil Rights Act of 1875 was unconstitutional due to the backlash of citizens standing up for what is right. To see in modern-day history, so many people in this country unite behind the horrific murder of a man publicly choked to death was a reminder that all is not lost. These are not "feel-good stories" at their foundation by any means; however, the response that these horrible situations garnered from average, everyday people is what is encouraging. Often, there can be beauty that comes after tragedy. The death of George Floyd happened at a time when the majority of the United States workforce was home due to the COVID-19 pandemic. A much different reaction happened after his death than the reactions I have seen in the past. You see, this death in this fashion is NOT a new occurrence amongst people that look like George Floyd. In fact, historically, there have been countless "George Floyds" for generations prior to this specific situation. What has not been the norm for generations is people of all walks of life in the United States standing up, protesting and demanding lawful accountability for a crime committed against someone like George Floyd. Having never seen thousands of people who do not look like me stand up for someone who does look like me was an amazing sight to behold, whether it should be or not. Some may say that it can be nothing but sad that, after 450 years, it seems like an amazing thing to witness people unite behind a wrongful murder that is the most recent of thousands that have happened for just as long. I get that; however, I believe that progress is still progress. This is how strides have been made over the history of this country, and quite frankly, why I am even able to discuss the things I'm discussing. Historically, I don't know that there have ever been thousands of protesters who were not black who rallied all over the country for almost 8 months after the death of a black man. Rallies where often times the crowd often has little to no faces of color in them are definitely something this country is not used to. A friend of mine told me that they believed the difference in the reaction to this murder was the country's inability to bury their head in the sand due to the pandemic. People who normally wouldn't see the news, normally wouldn't hear about the story about a black man wrongly murdered and people who had no clue that black people were now being and have been being wrongly murdered and assaulted by some in law enforcement for literally GENERATIONS. The exposure of this type of situation at this specific time became a screenshot that millions of Americans couldn't simply "unsee". After having conversations with several different individuals, it was stated to me time and time again that folks just didn't know or didn't realize what was going on because those were not the circumstances they had ever dealt with or the shoes that they walked in.

JUST TAKE FIVE STEPS OUTSIDE YOUR SHOES

The other day, I was having a conversation with an acquaintance of mine, and in the middle of our political banter, she paused and said, "Can I ask you a question?" "Sure!" I said, without hesitation. "Don't you think Kaepernick is a hypocrite? I mean, he did all of this talk about how racist the NFL is and how they treat players, similar to have slaves were treated so long ago. Why would he ever want to go back into the NFL or play? He must be motivated by money just like everyone else, and used the race card to justify his actions, and now he wants back in. If the NFL is so bad, shouldn't he just stay out of it instead of begging to get back in?"

I think she was surprised that I did not take offense to this at all. My first thought was as clear to me as the day was long. Here was someone trying to articulate and reason through a situation that they didn't understand in the first place; however, at least there was an open conversation to be had. It was actually very exciting to me to hear this perspective out loud and to have the opportunity to respond to it.

So, I said, "Just to be clear, your question is why would someone who trained their whole life to do one thing at the highest level want to continue with it? Why would someone who sacrificed high school life, college life, teenage life and young adulthood in order to commit everything to a sport, want to go back because the organization that runs it is unfair, unbalanced and inherently racist? Is that your question?" She then laughed and said that "When you say it like that, it sounds like I am asking a dumb question." I asked her if she had ever been an athlete. She had not. Have you ever given all that you had into driving for one goal with the belief that you can achieve it? She stated that she had not, as putting all your eggs in one basket was not a good idea. Then I asked she had ever been forced to exist in an environment that doesn't want your presence, but needs your presence? I was curious if she thought about what it would feel like to not be a part of the power structure that demanded she follow its rules, but have any say in the structure? She did understand somewhat in regard to being outside of the white male power structure.

Finally, I gave her a few examples of how being outside of the power structure leaves one powerless. "Do you remember when black people began criticizing tactics of the police department after the repeated killings of black people back-to-back right before Kaepernick started taking a knee? What changed? Do you remember when the public was told that taking a knee was not about the flag, not about veterans and not anti-America? Do you remember what the overwhelming response was from at least 30% of the country? It was "if you don't like it here, leave and go to another country.

These are the types of responses people of color get for demanding that something be done about what most people know is a problem nationwide. This is what you are told to do in the country that is the only one you have ever known? Take it and shut up, or leave? The place where you were born, went to elementary, middle and high school. The place where many served in the same military protecting freedoms, the right to speak out, vote and advocate for free change, are now told you are not patriotic, get out? Sounds like patriotism is only applicable based on how you look. At this point in our conversation, I could see that the statements were really starting to have an impact, so I completed the set of examples using myself. I asked, "Do you remember the conversations that we have had about my journey and experiences navigating through the industry we are in?" She acknowledged that she remembered. "What would you think if someone came to me because of the things that have happened to me at the hands of others and said, If you don't like how this business is run, don't complain about it, you should just get out?" It was at this point that I literally saw this individual put themselves in my shoes as best they could. I say this because the look on her face when it registered was unmistakable. A look that I know all too well when a painful truth resonates in one's spirit. Her response was, "I never thought about it like that. It never dawned on me that other than the difference in the job and salaries made, the football player experiences the same thing. I shared with her something my grandmother once said to me as a young man that sticks with me every day, no matter what happens. My grandmother said, "No matter what you do, you will always be black, and you should be proud of that. No matter how well you do in life, those in power will always see you as a nigger, don't subscribe to their definition of who they think you are. Know who you are, where you come from and how great you are. Don't let the world define you, define yourself." This is a perspective that you cannot accept and understand unless you are in these shoes or unless someone shares the experience with you. Needless to say, it was a very powerful conversation for both of us.

THE TALK

Putting yourself in someone else's shoes and “showing empathy” is a choice. It is not something anyone has to do. In most cases, if the situation doesn’t apply to you, empathy is typically not chosen. As human beings, we are inherently selfish in most aspects. When it comes to money and power, the concept of choosing not to be empathetic appears to double, if not triple, in people. The more people tend to acquire, the less they seem to be concerned about empathy or the shoes that others walk in. It’s as if money and power literally erode bits and pieces of our humanity away. Granted, I am speaking on the negative aspect of money and power, which does not apply to everyone. There are plenty of successful people who are very in touch with empathy and do not lose their humanity.

Conceptually, a part of what I believe has happened with some of the social atrocities we have seen over the last few years is the “not my problem” mindset. From Charlottesville to George Floyd, Brianna Taylor, Philando Castile, Oscar Grant and Michael Taylor back in the 80s in Indianapolis, Indiana or even the Watts riots that coincidentally stemmed from the same type of circumstances.

You would think that the reminders of the Emmet Till murder of a child 14 years old would have an impact and resonate with anyone who has a child, but it hasn’t. Here we are still plagued with the exact same behavior towards a specific group of people. When you think about how much could change if individuals simply took a moment to walk in the other person’s shoes, it’s incredible. What does it say about a society that doesn’t care enough to protect its women, and especially the children?

IS IT ALL HOPELESS?

Someone asked me what is to become of this country in the future and its future leaders? For some reason, this question took me to a very unexpected thought process. My response was "we neglect education, we do not honor law, we have forsaken freedoms, facts are now interchangeable, truth is now an ideology, protecting the innocent has taken a back seat to appeasing certain entities, politics over people is how we function, and morality, along with human decency, has eroded. For decades, all of these things have been taking place front and center for our children to experience, and we wonder why things are so bad now." I am often blown away at how surprised so many people are at things that transpire daily. The writing has been spray-painted all over the walls in capital letters for some time now. As my grandmother used to say, "even Ray Charles could see that coming."

We have become so self-destructive in our ways that we don't even celebrate those who come here to become American citizens anymore. Imagine that? A country that was built up by majorities of immigrants no longer celebrates welcoming and granting citizenship to immigrants freely. It seems the emphasis these days is on blaming those who want to come here, knowing they will endure our problems, while those who live here do not prioritize perpetuating prosperity. It feels like our true pride that bonded us regardless of our differences in this country has been chipped away bit by bit, year after year.

Both of my grandfathers were veterans, and even though they were not treated as men who served this country should have been, they still had pride in the roles they played to ensure the freedoms all people enjoy. They would tell me, "You have just as much right to everything in this country as anyone else." Regardless of a constitution and laws that were never written to benefit me, my patriarchs believed that I was entitled to all those same freedoms due to the price that my ancestors who came before me already paid. "This is your country, this is your home, no matter what," is what I was told.

I mention my grandfathers and the impact they had on me because I don't believe the type of pride they gave to me has continued to the next generation as a whole, not just for Black children, but for most children in this country. I believe this country has lost its way in so many facets that we cannot keep up anymore.

When I look at the United States now, I see a place that I don't recognize, yet at the same time, I see a place that has always been the same to me. I know that doesn't make sense and seems extremely contradictory, but allow me to expand on my statement.

In my lifetime, I have always known certain things to take place in this country. Police have always murdered and brutalized people of color. I've seen this since I was a child. The rights to equal opportunity under the law and access to freedoms for people of color have always been lesser or denied. This I have witnessed firsthand most of my life. The media and those in power have always painted the picture that the origin of this nation's crime and welfare problems is primarily due to people of color. This is mathematically impossible based on the population, which is probably why "per capita" was incorporated into all U.S. demographic data. (Statements like this didn't go over well in high school.) Manipulating numbers and percent's has always been a strength of those in power all around the world; America is no different. Last but not least, medical care and educational provisions have always been subpar at best for black people. Education and healthcare specifically are subjects that I could speak on for days in regard to the egregious actions and appropriations towards the black population; however, that is not the focal point. The point is, these are just a few things that millions of individuals like me have observed, lived with intimately and could speak to with clarity since our lives began. This is the side of this country that many of us know very well. We recognize her better than she recognizes herself most of the time. I came to realize quickly at a young age that what I recognize as the norms of this country for those who look like me are not the same norms that people who don't look like me recognize or experience daily.

What I don't recognize in this country leans on both sides of an emotional fence of positivity and negativity. Positively, I had never seen the country that would arrest, indict and convict a police officer for murder and brutality towards a black man. I have never witnessed a country that was outraged enough at watching a public execution by law enforcement that millions of white citizens stood up against it. A country that would elect a black man into the highest office in the land was something never thought possible. I don't recognize the country that would move forward with a vice president that was a black woman and then turn around and allow a Supreme Court justice to also be a black woman. There are many more things that I don't recognize about this country that have taken place, and quite frankly, I am very happy those things have transpired. One man's vision always has limitations. I'm so thankful that life moves beyond what any one person can fathom.

Unfortunately, I do recognize events like Charlottesville, I do recognize attacks like Ahmaud Arbery, mass school shootings, Breonna Taylor, church shootings, grocery store shootings, and so many more. It's normal to see certain politicians lobby for laws that are detrimental to minorities, redistricting voting zones, and at this point, it's not unfamiliar that voting rights are being taken away "yet again." It seems that many Americans forget that this song has already been played historically. Waiting for 10-12 hours to vote, polls are trying to close without allowing those in line to finish the process, and intimidation of voters is being used to deter them. I do recognize that isolating specific communities that vote and labeling their ballots as fraudulent is nothing new. Manipulating information and data to perpetuate a narrative negative towards specific groups of people is what I am used to seeing in this country. Americans do not realize that the subtle loss of these freedoms for some ends in the loss of those same freedoms for many more. We all must be aware that one type of change does not eliminate change on the opposite side of the coin. Accepting the negative norms of society has always been and will always be dangerous to everyone, regardless of what the masses believe. We Americans often believe that certain groups of people are monoliths, and their lives have no impact on change on other Americans. This is simply not true. The unfair expectations placed on others will always be exploited by those in power to apply to anyone they plan to control, including those who look like them but do not have the same power.

ALL THE EXPECTATIONS OF BLACK AMERICANS

"Why is there so much Black on Black crime? How can black people kill each other as much as they do? Why are there so many fatherless homes? Why don't black men take care of their kids? Everything black people get is given to them as a handout; it's all affirmative action. Why do we always blame the white person for holding us back? If you don't like it in America, you should leave instead of complaining about it. Why are black women so angry and bossy? All they care about is flashy clothes and cars. They should care more about their own communities instead of reacting only when another race does something against them! We are our own biggest enemy! Why are we like crabs in a barrel? All we care about is ourselves; we don't help our own kind. Why can't black people unify? They fight each other more than anyone else! Where does that arrogant attitude come from? Who does he/she think he is? Look at Mr. Joe college, who thinks he is better than everyone because he is going to school! Black communities used to care about each other in the past, but now there is no sense of community at all. All they do is use up all of the government assistance, waiting for handouts. Someone should cut off all welfare and make them work!

THE TALK

These are just a few of the comments that come from inside and outside of the black community on a daily basis. On the news, social media, workplace, train station, water coolers, restaurants, sporting events, households of all Americans, etc.

Before I dig into any of these questions, thoughts and concerns that have created engaging conversations between myself and many people, black, white, young, old and more, allow me to define something.

I am proud to call myself a black man. I recognize my strengths and weaknesses as a human being, a man and a person of color. I understand whose shoulders I stood on to thrive in life and where I come from, for better or worse. There are some mistakes I have made that are awful, and other things I've done that are amazing. My life has been full of joy, love and happiness all the while contending with fear, anger, sadness and hopeless moments of agony. I have been loved, feared, hated, celebrated, incarcerated, promoted, fired, accepted, denied, discriminated against, and given opportunity. Why say all of this? Hopefully, to show that as a human being, many of my experiences aren't too different from yours. The biggest difference is the narrative that has been associated with my experiences simply because of how I look. The example that acting as a "good parent" means I am the exception of what society says black men do in family, however, if I make a mistake as a parent, I am immediately defaulted to a no-good black father. Narratives matter even when we all do the same things.

The crazy thing is that I have had conversations about all the questions and statements listed above with black people, white people and other minorities. The horrible part is that so many have the same thoughts, but the great part is that after engaging in conversations, most see the questions differently and embrace another perspective. Sure, some have fictitiously acted like they get it when the truth is they really do not want to see any other perspective. Nothing can be done about someone dwelling in that space, as the only person who can impact that is their own self-awareness (which is so huge in any conversation and important to understand regarding who you are talking to).

Let's start with my conversations with other black men and women. There is an expectation that "we" should be better as a people in this country because of all that we have been through. All that our ancestors fought and died for, all the sacrifices and suffering they endured to give the next generation a chance to have better lives. How could we do all the things we see in our neighborhoods, all the things the news shows about us, disregard voting and gaining education that was at one point against the law to utilize? Stop playing the victim and blaming someone else for what we won't do for ourselves.

My last conversation about this was with someone close to me. We grew up together and have been able to establish a decent life for ourselves. Quite frankly, we've come a long way from how life began. Immediately, I could hear the hurt in his voice about how this country and the world perceive all of us. I cannot say that he was wrong about his indictments of many of us in our community; however, there was something I believed he was missing. My good friend had the belief that everything black people have endured for generations in this country meant that we could no longer be HUMAN BEINGS.

The thought that our pain supersedes our humanity, and we should not be impacted by circumstance, is a thought shared by so many. Because black people have survived horrific atrocities in this country, we expect perfection from ourselves as a form of protection. That is simply impossible. We believe that our people's crime rates should be different because so many crimes have been committed against us. Who would kill their fellow man after watching so many others kill him for generations? Well.... the answer to that is EVERY OTHER RACE IN THE WORLD. There is no group of people that does not kill each other. NONE!!! It is proven that most crimes committed are acts of proximity. That means that in all races and ethnicities, most crimes that are committed are against those who are within your reach. Your neighborhood, town, city, region, and country tend to outline an individual's reach to others and have been this way since mankind began. Vikings killed other Vikings, holy wars of neighboring countries and towns, Germans and Jews, the French Revolution, tribal wars for competing lands, hell, even cavemen killed each for perceived survival in the area they lived in. Suddenly, black people are supposed to be exempt from what the world has done since its inception of human beings? Why is there no other group of people labeled as their race-on-race crime?

Europeans have been killing each other for generations and that label has never been given. Iran, Iraq, Israel, Palestine, Russia, Ukraine, Germany, Poland, N Korea, S Korea, Syria, Ireland and on and on. We have had WW1 and WW2, and never were any of those countries labeled as white on white killing or crime, why?

Ultimately, the conversation with my friend turned into the understanding that accountability and the desire to improve and be better human beings are necessary; however, it also comes with grace for us to be just as human as anyone else. The circumstances black people have endured cannot replace the fact that we are human and flawed, just as every other human being, just more oppressed.

Now, my conversations with my white counterparts contain the same content; however, the revelation is received very differently. I can recall talking to a work acquaintance who, when I presented the same thing, it was as if Thor's hammer hit them in the head. Because she could never walk in my shoes, it hit her much harder when I pointed out the exact same behaviors that were acceptable and normal for people who looked like her but unbelievable for those who looked like me. She was confused and asking herself why she had a different meaning and expectation for the exact same actions white people executed. Why, if a young white teen shoplifted or tried weed, skipped school or threw rocks and broke a window, that was just being a boy, but if that same boy was black, he was a menace that should be locked up for decades as an adult. Why if a white assailant killed one or ten people, the goal was for law enforcement to apprehend him alive and then label him with mental challenges so that he could get help as part of his conviction. Meanwhile, if an individual who was black killed no one and reached for his phone, he would get 16 bullets. People would then say, "he should have complied."? I explained that one man can kill multiple people, have a weapon, and law enforcement try to talk him down; however, the black person who killed nobody deserves death for not complying because law enforcement are scared or filled with hate? The best part of this conversation and others just like it is that in the moment, the people I speak with are crystal clear on what is happening and what I am saying. Clearly, I cannot say that they retain this perception and maintain it at home or work with others, but i can say that the excuse of "I didn't know" or "I didn't think of it that way" is no longer a reality. It is not my belief that all white people or those of different races see me and other black people as non-human, but I do believe the system we live and function in subconsciously perpetuates this stigma and psychologically it does work. As an example, I can tell you that before Columbine high school shooting transpired, this country would have lost its mind regarding the killing of children in any capacity. We have gradually been desensitized that the death of children is an equal trade off to ensure that weapons and the dollars they generate in this country continue no matter who's hands they end up in or who dies. We have simply accepted this. Similarly, the shooting of unarmed black people by law enforcement or others has also been desensitized. To the effect that we can watch a man be executed on television via law enforcement by having his air supply cut off, and having so many people use reasons to justify it. Not because he killed someone, threatened the life of an officer, put a child at risk or endangered anyone, he died simply because the officer could kill him. We all watched George Floyd be reduced to something that was not human, that deserved to be killed for $20 of counterfeit currency. Meanwhile, men who execute Ponzi schemes, taking MILLIONS of dollars from other citizens get to live. The clarity of humanity, or lack thereof is very apparent when the narrative is examined and emphasized. This often brings those I am talking to close to the brink of tears as the reality I describe becomes undeniable.

None of this is to say that horrific crimes and behaviors by black Americans are acceptable and should not come with consequences. It is to say that the consequences should be at parity with those that others face for the exact same crimes. I stated this a few chapters ago: if a mother on crack in the 90s deserves to be in jail, having "crack babies," and that's the accountability, then the mother on opioids in the 2020s also deserves the same consequences. Rules are not supposed to change because crack arrests (notice I did not say use) were disproportionately black people, and opioid arrests are disproportionately white people. However, the rules did change. So much so that pharmaceutical companies were charged millions of dollars for the families; however, no one in the government was charged for ushering crack and drugs (that were not accessible to those dealers until the product was brought into the country) into the black community. I often use this example to isolate what humanity looks like to this nation. Let me be clear, most black people in this country are hardworking individuals who take care of their kids, make an honest living, care about their communities, abide by the law, have intelligent children, achieve great things and are proud of their family's contributions to this nation. With 45 million black people in the United States, the belief that most of us are either criminals or recipients of government assistance is simply not true.

Honestly, when this conversation comes up, I just use basic math rather than argue media tactics. Government programs get roughly a 1.3 trillion budget yearly. If every black person in this country were on welfare (I mean every one of us), it would take 28 million dollars per family to come close to using all the budgeted dollars allocated to welfare. It's actually about 17.2 million black adults and children that benefit from government programs; you do the math, but I digress.

When we talk about current state of black society in America, one cannot eliminate one of the biggest variables in the pursuit of excellence. After the Civil War, there were over 500 black towns across the United States. There are only 50 towns documented as being destroyed by mobs of individuals who killed men, women and children. We know there were many more that never made it into any courts or history books. These are towns where black people did exactly what the American dream required. They literally pulled themselves up by their own bootstrap with teachers, farmers, doctors, lawyers, churches, businesses and thriving communities. Time and time again, the efforts to live humane lives without bothering anyone else resulted in death and destruction, with lands stolen from those who cultivated them. Even Central Park in New York was destroyed and taken from a black community. The only communities that were left alone were the low-income areas that allowed black people to live with minimal resources to maintain the area. People were treated like animals and, over time, began to identify with this treatment. It was clear that any attempt to build a thriving community resulted in destruction, so many stopped trying to do so. Many Americans believe this is an excuse black people use, but how many Americans do you think would keep trying to build something that keeps being destroyed, costing their life? There is no empathy for black Americans but ask yourself about the empathy the country has whenever others face crisis. The great depression, earthquakes, tornadoes, fires, and even the Civil War. When the majority population suffers loss and has to start from scratch, many exceptions are made to provide support for them, not us. There was more empathy for the South that lost the Civil War, acquiring reparations to plantation owners for losing property (slaves). The brutal reality is that our humanity has always been nonexistent which has had far reaching systemic implications that have historically kept black Americans in a losing position, regardless of whether this country acknowledges it or not.

I find that this kind of conversation with those i speak with has more impact than simply going back and forth about every single question this chapter began with. Trying to fight each narrative and manipulated statistics becomes futile quickly. This type of dialogue also assigns true humanity to me and those who look like me which is the missing variable regarding black Americans historically. Truth is always the light for those who are willing to look and see it.

WE THE PEOPLE VS WE IN POWER (WHO ARE YOU)

One of the most memorable conversations I recall, was with someone I reported to as we got into a dialogue about making money. We were talking about politics, people and money. Now, mind you, this is a highly successful individual who doesn't have money concerns at all. That is not the case for me. I have many concerns financially, and by no means am I set for life. I do have a good life and I cannot complain, but I am far from the status of this person so I thought his perspective would be interesting to understand. We were discussing the likes and dislikes of people against each other when I told him that I thought people have more in common than they realize. People are pitted against each other in order for those in power to gain more power. He asked me what I meant, so I told him a story.

When my mother was a child, she would go to the grocery store with her parents, my grandparents. This wasn't the early 1900s, mind you; this was when MY MOTHER was a child. They could only enter the store from the back and only during specific times so that they did not shop at the same time as white customers. My mother always had disdain for the white families that could enter through the front door and shop whenever they liked. She knew the rules and understood that this is just how it was, however, it still made her feel less than human and very angry. In listening to my mother tell me the stories, I realized that her and my grandparents had a good relationship with the owner of the store. For some reason, this struck me as an odd situation, so I told her. She asked me why I thought it was odd and what I meant. I thought it was odd that the person who owned the store was able to make money off of the white family and the black family equally, even though the rules stated they were not equal. Regardless of the separation and segregation, he sold both groups the same items and benefitted financially regardless of how they saw each other. Either party had no idea if they were charged more than they should be; they were more engulfed in who was allowed in what door and when. Meanwhile, the store was undoubtedly in both groups' pockets, getting their dollars in lieu of the distraction of "who is treated better with privilege," taking precedent over the dollars they were being charged. In the end, the winner wasn't the white family with privilege or the black family with none; it was the store owner taking both families' revenue.

The white families thought they were on the same level as the store owner because of their status, which was acknowledged. However, the truth is, they were giving up their dollars to the person truly in power. For most families, black and white, this was the case with doctors, pharmacists, retail stores, grocery stores, car dealerships, real estate, and more. Those making money understood that most families spent the same amount of money regardless of race; however, if they were "made" to feel they were better than others, they never questioned what they were spending and why.

When I finished my story, the person I was talking to was shocked. He had never thought of it this way and always thought that his privilege was worth whatever the cost. He then began thinking of examples where exclusivity simply meant paying more dollars for services that were not necessarily more valuable. I explained to him that as long as those in power keep us divided, they can keep their hands in both of our pockets under fictitious beliefs. When the common family is united with others, the playing field is level for us all. Exploitation of us all is drastically reduced, and fair trade becomes more realistic. We all know that the average citizens carry the lion share of tax responsibility in this country; however, we are so distracted by going against each other that we often miss new tax laws that screw us all over. We don't realize that united, this wouldn't have happened to us. Why does this matter, you ask? It matters because more of us are in the same financial situation then we care to acknowledge. Low income living, struggling just above the poverty line, high interest rates, ridiculous costs for housing, unreasonable food prices at the grocery store and more are things we all endure regardless of race. What do you think would happen if "WE THE PEOPLE" came together about this? What would happen if the people realized that true balanced government is more important than "belonging to a side that acknowledges you, but still screws you over," while making you believe they are screwing over the other party?

Do you know what made Macolm X the most dangerous? It wasn't when he was with the Nation of Islam, pushing back against everything, talking about Kennedy being assassinated, or doing interviews, going against the police government. That is not when he was killed. He was killed when he left the Nation of Islam, traveled to other countries, and realized that outside of America, his beliefs were shared by both black and white people. That other countries acknowledged that America was in fact an oppressive country that should face consequences for its abuse of minorities.

When Malcolm returned and suddenly started talking to everyone, not just black people, that was when he became a true threat. Do you understand that someone who can unite the common person and show him that he is being used by those in power is someone who must be eliminated? When a person only represents one group of people, they will be labeled a socialist, communist or anti-American to keep them ostracised from their specific group. When a person appeals to black, white, Latino and women, they become a problem. They have now challenged the power structure and tools that drive capitalism which are also hate and separation. This also why the likes of Fred Hampton "the chairman," were killed so early. As long as he was perceived as a "black panther" type, those in power didn't worry too much about this young man, barely 21 years old. Once he was able to assemble Latinos, redneck and low-income whites, along with blacks in the same space, he became a problem. He was able to show those three groups of people that they were all in the same boat financially, just treated differently socially. By the time he was 22 yrs old, he was assassinated in his apartment while his pregnant wife watched. To be honest with you, when i share these kinds of conversations with black and white people, I always get the same look. The look of fear. It tells me that they know what I am saying is true, and it scares them to death. Progress doesn't come without pain, and we all know it. Yes, that is terrifying, I must admit, especially when you are not on the receiving end of social injustice. Who wants to trade in their own privilege in order to stop those in power from mistreating others? That's a hell of an ask to those who have watched minorities be oppressed, abused, incarcerated, misrepresented, and murdered. It is very clear how far those in power will go to keep that power. You can't find very many people who would willingly trade their own lives to be in a black person's shoes no matter how successful that black person is. The most important thing for the "people" to remember is this: at any time, those in power decide to treat you exactly the same as others who don't look like you, they absolutely can do so. Eventually, greed will require those in power to take even more from those who look like themselves to maintain power. Mathematically, it is financially impossible for the minorities in this country to carry the financial impact of keeping those in power wealthy. They must take more from the majority group in this country, and that does not stop at black people.

I don't know what happens moving forward, but I would encourage you to start having conversations with your fellow countrymen sooner than later. I am thoroughly enjoying having, learning, engaging and leaning into my conversations with others.

Hope to talk you soon!

DP

Resident population of the United States by race from 2000 to 2023

(in millions)

Search:

Records: 13

Characteristic	White	Black or African American	American Indian and Alaska Native	Asian	Native Hawaiian and Other Pacific Islander	Two or more races
2023	252.07	45.76	4.49	21.39	0.9	10.32
2022	251.6	45.4	4.41	20.9	0.88	10.06
2021	251.44	45.1	4.35	20.45	0.86	9.81
2020	251.64	44.91	4.3	20.22	0.85	9.6
2019	250.52	44.08	4.19	19.5	0.81	9.14
2018	249.96	43.73	4.15	19.13	0.79	8.92
2017	249.27	43.37	4.1	18.76	0.78	8.69
2016	248.41	42.97	4.05	18.28	0.77	8.46
2015	247.38	42.53	4	17.75	0.75	8.21
2014	246.35	42.09	3.95	17.2	0.74	7.97
2013	245.31	41.65	3.9	16.68	0.72	7.73
2012	244.35	41.23	3.85	16.2	0.71	7.5
2011	243.29	40.78	3.8	15.72	0.69	7.27

DOWNL

Source

Show

Show

Use As

Release

July 2024

Region

United St

Survey

July 2000

Supplen

Numbers

Hispanic

In 2018 t

Hispanic

Home • Crime in the U.S. • 2016 • Crime in the U.S. 2016 • Tables • Table 21

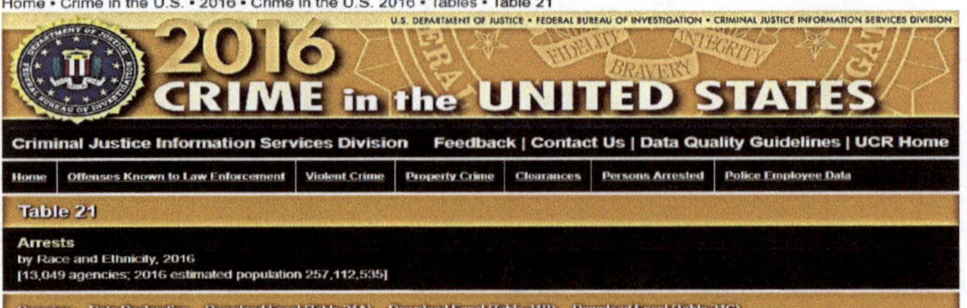

Table 21A

Offense charged	Total arrests: Race — Total	White	Black or African American	American Indian or Alaska Native	Asian	Native Hawaiian or Other Pacific Islander	Percent distribution[1] — Total	White	Black or African American	American Indian or Alaska Native	Asian	Native Hawaiian or Other Pacific Islander	Total arr… Ethnici… — Total[2]	Hispan… or Latino
TOTAL	8,421,481	5,858,330	2,263,112	171,185	103,244	25,610	100.0	69.6	26.9	2.0	1.2	0.3	6,647,012	1,221,0
Murder and nonnegligent manslaughter	9,374	4,192	4,935	108	109	30	100.0	44.7	52.6	1.2	1.2	0.3	6,882	1,3
Rape[3]	18,606	12,571	5,412	233	309	81	100.0	67.6	29.1	1.3	1.7	0.4	13,896	3,7
Robbery	76,267	33,095	41,562	663	659	288	100.0	43.4	54.5	0.9	0.9	0.4	60,116	12,6
Aggravated assault	304,626	191,205	101,432	6,374	4,678	937	100.0	62.8	33.3	2.1	1.5	0.3	250,762	61,0
Burglary	164,641	112,651	47,991	1,613	1,925	461	100.0	68.4	29.1	1.0	1.2	0.3	130,179	27,1
Larceny-theft	833,558	575,105	231,199	14,933	10,277	2,044	100.0	69.0	27.7	1.8	1.2	0.2	624,800	91,2
Motor vehicle theft	68,170	44,970	20,955	1,018	895	332	100.0	66.0	30.7	1.5	1.3	0.5	52,786	14,1
Arson	7,767	5,593	1,813	218	120	23	100.0	72.0	23.3	2.8	1.5	0.3	5,495	9
Violent crime[4]	408,873	241,063	153,341	7,378	5,755	1,336	100.0	59.0	37.5	1.8	1.4	0.3	331,656	78,862
Property crime[4]	1,074,136	738,319	301,958	17,782	13,217	2,860	100.0	68.7	28.1	1.7	1.2	0.3	813,260	133,393
Other assaults	853,493	556,871	267,764	15,505	10,511	2,842	100.0	65.2	31.4	1.8	1.2	0.3	665,711	121,3
Forgery and counterfeiting	44,831	29,375	14,308	290	752	106	100.0	65.5	31.9	0.6	1.7	0.2	35,180	5,5
Fraud	101,301	67,860	30,888	1,248	1,164	141	100.0	67.0	30.5	1.2	1.1	0.1	79,089	9,0
Embezzlement	12,592	7,732	4,512	104	209	35	100.0	61.4	35.8	0.8	1.7	0.3	10,178	1,2
Stolen property; buying, receiving, possessing	74,492	47,818	24,851	676	812	135	100.0	64.2	33.4	1.2	1.1	0.2	56,243	11,0
Vandalism	154,958	105,933	43,499	3,370	1,768	388	100.0	68.4	28.1	2.2	1.1	0.3	121,519	22,4
Weapons; carrying, possessing, etc.	124,150	69,414	51,898	1,135	1,401	302	100.0	55.9	41.8	0.9	1.1	0.2	97,279	22,7
Prostitution and commercialized vice	30,322	16,819	11,495	121	1,821	66	100.0	55.5	37.9	0.4	6.0	0.2	25,718	5,1
Sex offenses (except rape and prostitution)	40,292	28,837	9,949	633	749	124	100.0	71.6	24.7	1.6	1.9	0.3	32,402	8,1
Drug abuse violations	1,242,630	881,885	332,131	12,746	13,593	2,275	100.0	71.0	26.7	1.0	1.1	0.2	991,426	201,1
Gambling	2,905	1,308	1,405	8	167	17	100.0	45.0	48.4	0.3	5.7	0.6	1,958	5
Offenses against the family and children	69,546	46,661	20,265	2,065	519	36	100.0	67.1	29.1	3.0	0.7	0.1	55,805	6,3
Driving under the influence	798,012	655,648	108,881	14,700	15,969	2,814	100.0	82.2	13.6	1.8	2.0	0.4	657,336	148,5
Liquor laws	183,514	145,328	26,545	8,413	2,792	436	100.0	79.2	14.5	4.6	1.5	0.2	134,376	19,4
Drunkenness	299,248	228,784	43,948	23,043	3,046	427	100.0	76.5	14.7	7.7	1.0	0.1	266,894	64,3
Disorderly conduct	291,951	184,903	94,004	10,121	2,320	603	100.0	63.3	32.2	3.5	0.8	0.2	207,010	26,6
Vagrancy	19,755	13,033	6,063	412	234	13	100.0	66.0	30.7	2.1	1.2	0.1	16,265	2,6
All other offenses (except traffic)	2,567,092	1,775,423	704,293	50,666	26,136	10,574	100.0	69.2	27.4	2.0	1.0	0.4	2,024,802	327,5
Suspicion	440	154	135	143	5	3	100.0	35.0	30.7	32.5	1.1	0.7	239	
Curfew and loitering law violations	26,948	15,162	10,979	426	304	77	100.0	56.3	40.7	1.6	1.1	0.3	22,666	4,9

- [1] Because of rounding, the percentages may not add to 100.0.

Home • Crime in the U.S. • 2017 • Crime in the U.S. 2017 • Tables • Table 43

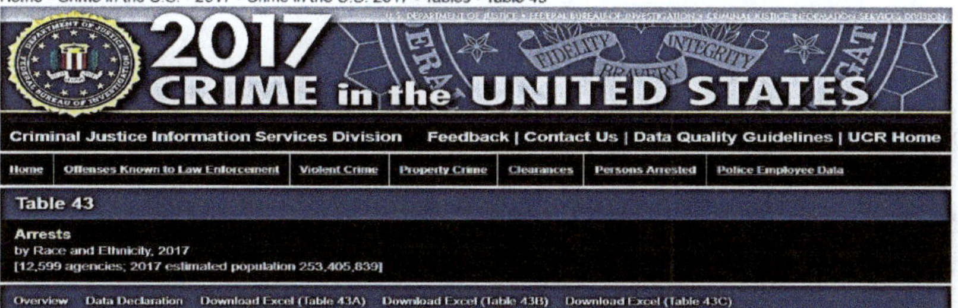

Table 43A

	Total arrests												Total arre	
	Race						Percent distribution[1]						Ethnicity	
Offense charged	Total	White	Black or African American	American Indian or Alaska Native	Asian	Native Hawaiian or Other Pacific Islander	Total	White	Black or African American	American Indian or Alaska Native	Asian	Native Hawaiian or Other Pacific Islander	Total[2]	Hispanic or Latino
TOTAL	8,162,849	5,626,140	2,221,697	196,908	97,049	21,055	100.0	68.9	27.2	2.4	1.2	0.3	6,584,533	1,190,67
Murder and nonnegligent manslaughter	9,468	4,188	5,025	108	127	20	100.0	44.2	53.1	1.1	1.3	0.2	7,031	1,46
Rape[3]	18,063	12,187	5,182	322	307	65	100.0	67.5	28.7	1.8	1.7	0.4	14,025	3,78
Robbery	73,764	32,128	40,024	679	664	269	100.0	43.6	54.3	0.9	0.9	0.4	59,680	12,72
Aggravated assault	302,941	188,087	101,513	7,531	4,881	929	100.0	62.1	33.5	2.5	1.6	0.3	255,056	61,10
Burglary	154,970	104,671	46,227	1,968	1,710	394	100.0	67.5	29.8	1.3	1.1	0.3	123,671	24,87
Larceny-theft	740,546	501,231	215,650	13,242	8,770	1,653	100.0	67.7	29.1	1.8	1.2	0.2	563,359	78,92
Motor vehicle theft	70,617	46,621	21,415	1,308	980	293	100.0	66.0	30.3	1.9	1.4	0.4	55,723	14,52
Arson	7,086	5,051	1,788	112	116	19	100.0	71.3	25.2	1.6	1.6	0.3	5,594	1,07
Violent crime[4]	404,236	236,590	151,744	8,640	5,979	1,283	100.0	58.5	37.5	2.1	1.5	0.3	335,792	79,078
Property crime[4]	973,219	657,574	285,080	16,630	11,576	2,359	100.0	67.6	29.3	1.7	1.2	0.2	748,347	119,392
Other assaults	822,671	534,188	258,542	17,062	10,371	2,508	100.0	64.9	31.4	2.1	1.3	0.3	658,243	118,92
Forgery and counterfeiting	43,203	28,130	13,980	386	619	88	100.0	65.1	32.4	0.9	1.4	0.2	34,659	5,33
Fraud	95,997	63,908	29,556	1,256	1,174	103	100.0	66.6	30.8	1.3	1.2	0.1	75,632	8,83
Embezzlement	12,437	7,441	4,683	96	190	27	100.0	59.8	37.7	0.8	1.5	0.2	10,189	1,24
Stolen property; buying, receiving, possessing	76,477	48,607	25,585	1,034	940	311	100.0	63.6	33.5	1.4	1.2	0.4	58,425	11,35
Vandalism	145,934	99,818	40,861	3,265	1,681	309	100.0	68.4	28.0	2.2	1.2	0.2	117,580	21,54
Weapons; carrying, possessing, etc.	128,009	68,787	56,143	1,357	1,400	322	100.0	53.7	43.9	1.1	1.1	0.3	101,538	23,12
Prostitution and commercialized vice	28,229	15,812	10,605	116	1,610	86	100.0	56.0	37.6	0.4	5.7	0.3	24,578	5,09
Sex offenses (except rape and prostitution)	37,518	26,615	9,355	691	741	116	100.0	70.9	24.9	1.8	2.0	0.3	31,424	7,63
Drug abuse violations	1,262,660	889,030	342,513	15,038	13,691	2,388	100.0	70.4	27.1	1.2	1.1	0.2	1,019,770	201,85
Gambling	2,493	955	1,294	20	183	41	100.0	38.3	51.9	0.8	7.3	1.6	1,558	382
Offenses against the family and children	71,656	46,926	20,106	4,067	534	23	100.0	65.5	28.1	5.7	0.7	*	57,018	6,67
Driving under the influence	755,726	617,443	105,585	15,950	14,294	2,454	100.0	81.7	14.0	2.1	1.9	0.3	627,315	140,91
Liquor laws	157,285	122,929	22,095	9,705	2,347	209	100.0	78.2	14.0	6.2	1.5	0.1	117,267	15,70
Drunkenness	287,985	212,908	41,073	30,632	2,931	441	100.0	73.9	14.3	10.6	1.0	0.2	267,218	57,52
Disorderly conduct	273,664	172,098	87,094	11,832	2,232	408	100.0	62.9	31.8	4.3	0.8	0.1	201,451	24,68
Vagrancy	18,453	12,609	5,148	473	209	14	100.0	68.3	27.9	2.6	1.1	0.1	15,017	2,19
All other offenses (except traffic)	2,540,842	1,750,366	700,984	57,979	24,046	7,467	100.0	68.9	27.6	2.3	0.9	0.3	2,061,185	335,00
Suspicion	669	250	148	258	7	6	100.0	37.4	22.1	38.6	1.0	0.9	468	4
Curfew and loitering law violations	23,486	13,156	9,523	421	294	92	100.0	56.0	40.5	1.8	1.3	0.4	19,859	4,12

- [1] Because of rounding, the percentages may not add to 100.0

Home • Crime in the U.S. • 2018 • Crime in the U.S. 2018 • Tables • Table 43

U.S. DEPARTMENT OF JUSTICE • FEDERAL BUREAU OF INVESTIGATION • CRIMINAL JUSTICE INFORMATION SERVICES DIVISION

2018 CRIME in the UNITED STATES

FIDELITY BRAVERY INTEGRITY

Criminal Justice Information Services Division | Feedback | Contact Us | Data Quality Guidelines | UCR Home

Home | Offenses Known to Law Enforcement | Violent Crime | Property Crime | Clearances | Persons Arrested | Police Employee Data

Table 43

Arrests
by Race and Ethnicity, 2018
[12,212 agencies; 2018 estimated population 247,752,415]

Overview | Data Declaration | Download Excel (Table 43A) | Download Excel (Table 43B) | Download Excel (Table 43C)

Table 43A

	Total arrests												Total arres	
	Race						Percent distribution[1]						Ethnicity	
Offense charged	Total	White	Black or African American	American Indian or Alaska Native	Asian	Native Hawaiian or Other Pacific Islander	Total	White	Black or African American	American Indian or Alaska Native	Asian	Native Hawaiian or Other Pacific Islander	Total[2]	Hispanic or Latino
TOTAL	7,710,900	5,319,654	2,115,381	164,430	92,737	18,698	100.0	69.0	27.4	2.1	1.2	0.2	6,343,684	1,191,33
Murder and nonnegligent manslaughter	8,957	3,953	4,778	105	94	27	100.0	44.1	53.3	1.2	1.0	0.3	7,050	1,47
Rape[3]	18,776	12,794	5,376	267	289	50	100.0	68.1	28.6	1.4	1.5	0.3	15,316	4,09
Robbery	66,789	29,025	36,187	676	641	260	100.0	43.5	54.2	1.0	1.0	0.4	57,048	12,82
Aggravated assault	298,040	184,527	100,393	6,736	5,078	1,306	100.0	61.9	33.7	2.3	1.7	0.4	254,614	65,05
Burglary	134,542	91,581	39,617	1,590	1,422	332	100.0	68.1	29.4	1.2	1.1	0.2	114,027	23,20
Larceny-theft	669,983	448,193	201,086	11,987	7,324	1,393	100.0	66.9	30.0	1.8	1.1	0.2	540,174	78,10
Motor vehicle theft	69,002	44,512	22,305	1,151	818	216	100.0	64.5	32.3	1.7	1.2	0.3	56,263	14,39
Arson	6,946	4,938	1,740	137	101	30	100.0	71.1	25.1	2.0	1.5	0.4	5,790	1,05
Violent crime[4]	392,562	230,299	146,734	7,784	6,102	1,643	100.0	58.7	37.4	2.0	1.6	0.4	334,028	83,441
Property crime[4]	880,473	589,224	264,748	14,865	9,665	1,971	100.0	66.9	30.1	1.7	1.1	0.2	716,254	116,753
Other assaults	794,787	512,025	254,360	15,711	10,348	2,343	100.0	64.4	32.0	2.0	1.3	0.3	654,150	125,00
Forgery and counterfeiting	37,724	25,140	11,637	335	548	64	100.0	66.6	30.8	0.9	1.5	0.2	31,565	5,30
Fraud	89,610	58,572	28,387	1,419	1,088	144	100.0	65.4	31.7	1.6	1.2	0.2	74,521	9,63
Embezzlement	11,174	6,923	3,955	122	159	15	100.0	62.0	35.4	1.1	1.4	0.1	9,252	1,19
Stolen property; buying, receiving, possessing	69,874	44,179	23,661	881	819	334	100.0	63.2	33.9	1.3	1.2	0.5	57,379	11,27
Vandalism	134,794	91,176	38,887	2,949	1,552	230	100.0	67.6	28.8	2.2	1.2	0.2	112,716	21,47
Weapons; carrying, possessing, etc.	126,332	68,756	54,715	1,094	1,390	377	100.0	54.4	43.3	0.9	1.1	0.3	100,312	23,66
Prostitution and commercialized vice	23,502	12,928	9,109	95	1,309	61	100.0	55.0	38.8	0.4	5.6	0.3	21,484	4,37
Sex offenses (except rape and prostitution)	35,157	25,338	8,403	587	751	78	100.0	72.1	23.9	1.7	2.1	0.2	28,928	7,39
Drug abuse violations	1,234,178	871,295	333,113	14,148	13,345	2,277	100.0	70.6	27.0	1.1	1.1	0.2	1,044,789	211,69
Gambling	2,465	1,000	1,198	11	205	51	100.0	40.6	48.6	0.4	8.3	2.1	1,390	341
Offenses against the family and children	64,357	43,371	18,530	1,895	510	51	100.0	67.4	28.8	2.9	0.8	0.1	51,589	5,99
Driving under the influence	736,644	597,919	108,703	13,150	14,323	2,549	100.0	81.2	14.8	1.8	1.9	0.3	604,136	147,22
Liquor laws	128,453	100,687	18,743	6,973	1,876	174	100.0	78.4	14.6	5.4	1.5	0.1	102,624	15,97
Drunkenness	251,490	193,042	37,781	17,412	2,825	430	100.0	76.8	15.0	6.9	1.1	0.2	233,325	52,49
Disorderly conduct	248,716	158,533	78,192	9,770	1,926	295	100.0	63.7	31.4	3.9	0.8	0.1	186,261	24,55
Vagrancy	18,048	12,823	4,458	482	261	24	100.0	71.0	24.7	2.7	1.4	0.1	16,649	2,55
All other offenses (except traffic)	2,413,408	1,666,825	663,086	54,410	23,550	5,537	100.0	69.1	27.5	2.3	1.0	0.2	1,947,281	317,92
Suspicion	432	237	129	65	1	0	100.0	54.9	29.9	15.0	0.2	0.0	390	1
Curfew and loitering law violations	16,720	9,362	6,852	272	184	50	100.0	56.0	41.0	1.6	1.1	0.3	14,661	3,03

Home • Crime in the U.S. • 2019 • Crime in the U.S. 2019 • Tables • Table 43

U.S. DEPARTMENT OF JUSTICE • FEDERAL BUREAU OF INVESTIGATION • CRIMINAL JUSTICE INFORMATION SERVICES DIVISION

2019 CRIME in the UNITED STATES

FIDELITY BRAVERY INTEGRITY

Criminal Justice Information Services Division | Feedback | Contact Us | Data Quality Guidelines | UCR Home

Home | Offenses Known to Law Enforcement | Violent Crime | Property Crime | Clearances | Persons Arrested | Police Employee Data

Table 43

Arrests

by Race and Ethnicity, 2019

[10,831 agencies; 2019 estimated population 229,735,355]

Overview | Data Declaration | Download Excel (Table 43A) | Download Excel (Table 43B) | Download Excel (Table 43C)

Table 43A

	Total arrests												Total arres	
	Race						Percent distribution[1]						Ethnicity	
Offense charged	Total	White	Black or African American	American Indian or Alaska Native	Asian	Native Hawaiian or Other Pacific Islander	Total	White	Black or African American	American Indian or Alaska Native	Asian	Native Hawaiian or Other Pacific Islander	Total[2]	Hispanic or Latino
TOTAL	6,816,975	4,729,290	1,815,144	164,852	86,733	20,956	100.0	69.4	26.6	2.4	1.3	0.3	5,896,059	1,126,80
Murder and nonnegligent manslaughter	7,964	3,650	4,078	125	83	28	100.0	45.8	51.2	1.6	1.0	0.4	6,474	1,34
Rape[3]	16,599	11,588	4,427	249	276	59	100.0	69.8	26.7	1.5	1.7	0.4	14,172	3,94
Robbery	56,305	25,143	29,677	635	568	282	100.0	44.7	52.7	1.1	1.0	0.5	50,705	12,00
Aggravated assault	274,376	169,467	91,164	7,192	4,902	1,651	100.0	61.8	33.2	2.6	1.8	0.6	243,279	62,42
Burglary	118,843	81,104	34,188	1,728	1,464	359	100.0	68.2	28.8	1.5	1.2	0.3	105,558	21,98
Larceny-theft	592,679	393,226	178,937	11,718	7,133	1,665	100.0	66.3	30.2	2.0	1.2	0.3	502,776	74,22
Motor vehicle theft	57,278	38,719	16,409	1,213	721	216	100.0	67.6	28.6	2.1	1.3	0.4	50,482	12,72
Arson	6,291	4,453	1,553	121	125	39	100.0	70.8	24.7	1.9	2.0	0.6	5,460	1,02
Violent crime[4]	355,244	209,848	129,346	8,201	5,829	2,020	100.0	59.1	36.4	2.3	1.6	0.6	314,630	79,71
Property crime[4]	775,091	517,502	231,087	14,780	9,443	2,279	100.0	66.8	29.8	1.9	1.2	0.3	664,276	109,95
Other assaults	703,534	455,901	219,400	16,037	9,907	2,289	100.0	64.8	31.2	2.3	1.4	0.3	608,510	115,06
Forgery and counterfeiting	32,100	21,537	9,668	338	501	56	100.0	67.1	30.1	1.1	1.6	0.2	28,277	4,78
Fraud	78,698	51,861	24,041	1,424	1,208	164	100.0	65.9	30.5	1.8	1.5	0.2	68,160	9,98
Embezzlement	9,886	5,983	3,587	114	179	23	100.0	60.5	36.3	1.2	1.8	0.2	8,271	1,09
Stolen property; buying, receiving, possessing	63,035	38,751	21,998	1,108	825	353	100.0	61.5	34.9	1.8	1.3	0.6	54,930	10,33
Vandalism	126,161	86,360	34,670	3,198	1,598	335	100.0	68.5	27.5	2.5	1.3	0.3	109,856	21,33
Weapons; carrying, possessing, etc.	108,847	60,494	45,530	1,129	1,247	447	100.0	55.6	41.8	1.0	1.1	0.4	92,892	22,08
Prostitution and commercialized vice	19,811	10,074	8,370	73	1,205	89	100.0	50.9	42.2	0.4	6.1	0.4	18,191	3,50
Sex offenses (except rape and prostitution)	28,627	21,360	5,903	596	668	100	100.0	74.6	20.6	2.1	2.3	0.3	25,184	7,02
Drug abuse violations	1,052,101	748,874	274,670	14,098	11,857	2,602	100.0	71.2	26.1	1.3	1.1	0.2	946,784	194,65
Gambling	1,895	1,081	553	13	214	34	100.0	57.0	29.2	0.7	11.3	1.8	1,682	43
Offenses against the family and children	58,042	38,196	16,454	2,821	493	78	100.0	65.8	28.3	4.9	0.8	0.1	49,402	6,44
Driving under the influence	646,607	526,928	90,888	12,373	13,071	3,347	100.0	81.5	14.1	1.9	2.0	0.5	549,292	145,12
Liquor laws	109,887	85,350	17,077	5,657	1,651	152	100.0	77.7	15.5	5.1	1.5	0.1	90,033	14,80
Drunkenness	218,095	164,797	32,255	18,238	2,431	374	100.0	75.6	14.8	8.4	1.1	0.2	206,492	46,63
Disorderly conduct	208,690	132,676	64,049	9,811	1,820	334	100.0	63.6	30.7	4.7	0.9	0.2	164,645	22,89
Vagrancy	15,952	10,763	4,497	473	201	18	100.0	67.5	28.2	3.0	1.3	0.1	14,779	2,10
All other offenses (except traffic)	2,192,791	1,532,998	577,689	54,049	22,248	5,807	100.0	69.9	26.3	2.5	1.0	0.3	1,870,588	306,54
Suspicion	1,316	1,008	257	49	2	0	100.0	76.6	19.5	3.7	0.2	0.0	410	3
Curfew and loitering law violations	10,565	6,948	3,155	272	135	55	100.0	65.8	29.9	2.6	1.3	0.5	8,775	2,25

www.ingramcontent.com/pod-product-compliance
Lightning Source LLC
Chambersburg PA
CBHW062135020426
42335CB00013B/1220

* 9 7 8 1 9 7 0 3 7 9 0 6 8 *